Dead Angel

By **John Clark**

"DEAD ANGEL"
By John Clark

**Edited and with a forward
By Jim Schock**

Dead Angel
Table Of Contents

Introduction
by Clifford "Tiff" Garcia,
Jerry Garcia's brother and a personal friend of the author.

FORWARD

By Jim Schock

The world knew Jerry Garcia. The world mourned his death. Deadheads and dope-heads and a couple of generations of people knew Jerry Garcia. They knew him from the Haight, and the concerts and the records. Since his death, there have been books about Jerry Garcia; written by people whose lives he touched in one way or another. But only one man can write about Jerry's childhood and early years, about his curiosity, about the private, forever-gone blue-blue skies days of comic books, tree houses, and adventures with wooden swords that played out on the one-block neighborhood where he grew up. The halcyon days when each morning promised an adventure, each night untroubled sleep.

No one knew Jerry Garcia, except one man, a man who shared those days, those adventures, that friendship.

That man is John Clark.

When you meet someone and both of you are about five years old, and you - share the rites of childhood together, you establish a bond that is strong and lasting. The bond between John Clark and Jerry Garcia was constructed of that kind of perma-nent glue. Remember your best friend, the one you built forts with? The one who liked the same comic books you did? The one whose childhood was as rocky and dark as your own? Once you have those kinds of people in your life you never lose them, ever.

This book is about a friendship like that. This isn't a story about sex, drugs and rock and roll, or about million dollar record deals, business empires or legal battles over fabulous estates. It's not even about fame, legends, or social icons. This is a story about two friends, one who became world-famous, legendary, and a lasting icon of a social age, while the other became an actor, a lobbyist, and rode a motor-cycle, joined a motorcycle club called the Presidents, and rode through a torn, tor-mented time of recent American history with Jerry's music pounding in the back-ground.

Their friendship was forged on the streets of San Francisco, and tempered by common enemies, broken families, times of poverty, daily turmoil and a lot of mutual trust and respect. Friendships like that endure until death do they part.
And for the survivor, there are the sweet memories of youth, brightly burnished, forever glinting in the sun. For the rest of us, there's lightning and laughter in the dark nights of our sadness.

Jim Schock
Mill Valley, CA
Spring 2000

CHAPTER ONE
HARRINGTON STREET, SAN FRANCISCO, 1947

1947 – America after WWII. The world was changing faster than ever before. Pan American World Airways announced the first around-the-world airline flight. The trip required 13 days and $1,700. Jackie Robinson broke the major league color barrier. Joe Louis was still defending his world heavyweight title. Golf's top money-winner was Jimmy Demaret; his take was $27,936.83.

The Marshall Plan to rebuild Europe was proposed. Among the books published in 1947: The Big Sky, by A.B. Guthrie; Tales of the South Pacific, by James Michener; The Wayward Bus, by John Steinbeck; and I, the Jury, by a former comic book writer, Mickey Spillane. Broadway's first Tony Awards were presented, and Captain Chuck Yeager broke the sound barrier.

You're six years old and you meet a kid who's five years old. He likes the same comic books you do, and you discover a lot of other stuff you have in common. Then you find out he lives across the street from you, so you become the best of friends and that friendship lasts forever. Jerry Garcia was five, mostly alone in the world and so was I. We knew each other 50 years and that didn't come close to being long enough.

In 1947 I was six, and Harrington Street, where I lived, was a world unto itself. It still is. And it's still only one block long. It's still located in a section of San Francisco known as the Excelsior, a neighborhood that makes up part of the Outer Mission district. We were about three miles from downtown San Francisco – downtown being defined as Union Square and the Financial District or Civic Center. If you can think of Flatbush as a part of Brooklyn – it's like that. At one end, Harrington Street is attached to Mission Street, which runs from the Ferry Building all the way to the city limits, and it's the longest street in San Francisco.

From the Excelsior we could see Mt. Davidson, the hilltop where a 105-foot cross tower over our neighborhood. As kids we assumed it was there to guard over us, and the light that illuminated it at night spilled across the houses and vacant lots of our one-street world.

The block wasn't distinguished in any way. It was another strip of working-class people doing their best to get by in a postwar world. The families were Italian, Irish, and Mexican, and in those days people didn't move around much. Several generations remained in the neighborhood, often living in the same house their entire lives. The children of the block shared the street and their lives and it was here that I met Jerry Garcia. We met the way Life intends friends to meet for the first time – by accident.

Jerry lived at 87 Harrington, the last house on the south side next to Alemany

Boulevard. It was a large stucco house with a big side yard. I lived at 32 Harrington, the seventh house down from Mission on the north side of the street in one of those Northern California Victorian houses that retained a touch of Gothic.

My family and I lived on the second floor. The landlord was Mr. Sullivan, who occupied the ground floor. Two doors up was an Italian bakery and, as you might expect, the smell of fresh bread and pizza was a permanent part of the air we breathed. Even the faintest hint of fresh-baked bread or crisping pizza dough sends Harrington Street and San Francisco, me back to 1947.

Even though the memories are now in soft-focus and fog-shrouded, life in our one-block world was by no means easy. Most of the families there were unable to do more than smile thinly at any notion of living the American Dream – the thing that returning GIs had said they had fought for as recently as two years earlier.

Adults concentrated fiercely on being able to provide for their families, many of which were shattered by divorce, abandonment, or death. All of us lived with odd combinations of relatives, trying to find comfort and meaning in a world that seemed void of such qualities.

As kids, of course, we wore the innocent blinders childhood provides. There was no denying it was a harsh, real world, but we survived and even thrived in our self-constructed world of make-believe. We had hideaways, and we had book and radio serial-inspired games, days of sunlight and fog, into which we created our adventures. Unlike today, adults were happy to have us out from underfoot, and in that era of permissiveness we pursued childhood eagerly and earnestly.

Meeting the Little Kid.

At 2400 Mission Street stood a community landmark, the Central Drugstore. I spent many hours amidst the strange smells and exotic products of the old pharmacy. OK, some products were not so exotic. One reason for my extended hours there was because I had discovered a hidden corner where, out of sight of the owner, I could read all the comic books. It was a safe haven in a world of comic book heroes, where I would linger for hours to avoid going home to my alcoholic stepfather or to my abusive mother.

I considered this alcove in the Central Drugstore my private territory so it was with a sense of proprietorship that I was startled one day to find this little fat kid in my private spot. My territory. My turf. It was Jerry Garcia. He was five years old.

"Hi," I said, unwilling to create too much of a scene, lest the owner run us both off, discover my secret place and fill it with a display of lunch buckets or something.

"You like comic books, too?" he asked.

"I sure do," I replied.

We began to talk to each other in whispers to avoid detection by the owner or one of the clerks, and in the space of those few minutes a permanent bond was established, never to be broken. It helped that even at age six, I could plainly see Jerry obviously wasn't eager to go home. It might start with liking the same comic books, but kids find out a lot about each other right away. There's no false modesty or hidden agendas to get in the way. It's two-way curiosity, simple questions, and straight- forward answers.

Jerry told me he had been uprooted from his home in the Crocker-Amazon District and lived with his grandmother on Harrington Street.

"Hey, that's my street, too!"

He also told me he lived with his older brother, Cliff, and they didn't get along too well. I could understand that because I didn't get along at all with my younger half-brother. He said he didn't see his mother very often. I nodded. For a minute our lives were so much alike, I thought we could probably go home to each other's house and no one would notice.

The sun was going down as we headed back to Harrington Street. We were new best friends, and I thought I knew everything there was to know about my new buddy Jerry, because from the summit of my six years, I knew that at age five, there isn't that much that can happen to a kid younger than me. Suddenly Jerry stopped. He just stopped walking and stood there in the middle of the sidewalk and looked at me and said, "I saw my father die." I blinked. "Right in front of my own eyes."

I looked at him, and his brown eyes seemed to hold a great sadness. For the next 50 years, whenever I saw Jerry, some of the sadness I saw in his eyes that day seemed to linger on.

The Big Lot.

To the children of the Excelsior, our tiny neighborhood always seemed ripe for big adventures. Well, to the big to single-digit kids at least. Harrington Street featured modest homes, including an occasional vacant house. There were two vacant lots. One we called the Big Lot, and it had all of the fun stuff, including a tree house. It was the playground of choice for every kid in the neighborhood. Here childhood friendships were established, fights were conducted, and rivalries were born, and it was nothing less than the hub of our universe.

I headed for the Big Lot every day after school. So did all the other guys, because none of us wanted to miss anything, and the Big Lot was where everything was going to happen. One of the reasons for this was due to the fact that it was the domain of the older kids, those mature specimens, fifth and sixth graders, who were forever telling us smaller kids to scram.

When we scrammed, it was to our refuge, the Little Lot. The Little Lot was a lot less interesting, but it was ours. Childhood was full of age discrimination. Maybe it still is. We called them the Big Kids, and they called us the Little Kids, but the meanings of the phrases went far beyond the simple words that expressed them. Jerry and I were Little Kids. Jerry's brother, Cliff, was one of the Big Kids.

As often happens with those in power, the Big Kids decided to expand their territory. In doing so, they took over the Little Lot. Our Little Lot. They dug in; built a fort of two-by-fours; brush, cardboard with gun slits in the walls that allowed them to shoot at us with their BB guns. It may seem hard to understand now, but exchange of BB gun fire was a common occurrence in those days. Despite the universal warning of mothers everywhere, "You'll put your eye out with those things," no one lost an eye. If you got hit on or near your face, the last thing you did was tell your mother. The concept of "grounding" had not arrived in our parents' lives, but the concept of "pounding" had. The society of kids is stronger than you think.

If the will of those in power is to expand their borders, it is the will of the oppressed to organize in their defense. So that's what we did. The only organization of any type we knew anything about came from the movies, so we organized an army. I forget how, but we procured a motley array of confederate hats, and by default became the Rebel Army. In keeping with this theme, we designated the Big Kids the Union Army.

One of our recruits was a neighborhood kid we called High Pockets, because he wore his pants up high around his waist, thereby accentuating his bright, white socks. He was "a brain" and he had an electric train set at his house. In later life, he avoided music and motorcycles – the paths Jerry and I would take – but he went on to become a scientist, ensuring that he had the last laugh on his childhood buddies. His name was Jim Sweeney, and today he'd be classified as a nerd, and would be worth about a billion dollars. Back then, Jim became General of our Confederate Army, and he accepted his responsibilities with great seriousness. He would have us march endlessly, carrying broomstick rifles, hut-two, hut-two. When we grew tired, our efforts to convince him soldiers didn't win battles by marching, but by other means, fell on deaf ears. Jim recruited me as a Sergeant, and he recruited Jerry as a Private. Now we had a chain of command.

I took orders from General Jim. Being the youngest, Private Jerry took orders from General Jim, too, and from Sergeant John. The little fat kid with the sad eyes tried his best to be a good soldier, even though his rifle was taller than he was. He worked hard because he wanted to be part of our assault force when we liberated the Harrington Street Little Lot. Like the rest of us, Jerry also had huge ambitions to confiscate the weapons of war, those Red Ryder BB guns presently being held by our enemy. During one battle planning session, we decided that when we regained the Little Lot, disarmed the Union Army, thus arming ourselves, we would proceed to liberate the Big Lot, taking command and control of the tree house. Victory would be ours, and we would be in charge. It never occurred to us our plans, which began with liberation, ended with tyranny, a scheme matching that of despots and tyrants known throughout history. We just wanted to get the best of the Big Kids.

While we were planning in our imaginary War Room, General Jim decided we needed a lookout whose job it would be to spy on the big kids in the big lot. We were wary of attacking them, even though we would have outnumbered them, because they possessed superior weaponry – BB guns. Through the chain of command, the general ordered me, and I ordered Private Jerry Garcia, to climb the palm tree at the edge of the lot in order to spy on the enemy encampment. Jerry took one look at the tree and stepped back.

"Do I have to, sergeant?" he asked. Jerry wasn't fond of heights.

"It's an order, private," I answered. "I expect discipline from my men!"

With that Jerry swallowed, and began to shinny up the tree. It wasn't easy, but he made it up about 10 feet (which seemed like a lot more at the time), then, with a cry, lost his grip, and I watched with horror as he crashed to the ground with a thudding sound that seemed to shake the ground under my feet. I was certain Private Jerry Garcia had killed himself. I rushed over to him to confirm my worst fear.

"Jerry! Are you all right?" I screamed. The only thing I knew to do was what we'd all learned in the movies about such situations. I tried shaking him. I patted his cheek, and I looked around desperately for some water to throw on his face, because that always worked in picture shows. The other little kids came running over. They had seen him fall and they thought he was dead, too. He didn't move. Not a muscle. My friend, Jerry Garcia, our best private, had just died in the line of duty. I began to cry over the death of my friend, whose life had ended because of an order I gave. My tears splashed down on his face, and they must have been miracle tears, because his eyes suddenly blinked open and then became all white as they rolled around.

He had the wind knocked out of him, something we'd heard about, but never witnessed in real life. He had also raised a bump on his head, but he was back to normal after a few minutes. Since he wasn't dead, the other little kids drifted away, and some of them seemed disappointed. It did not occur to me to put him in for a Purple Heart.

After Jerry's mishap, we abandoned the idea of a lookout, because no one would try climbing the palm tree after what happened to Private Garcia.

We did not give up our plan to liberate the Little Lot. We armed ourselves with stick and brooms and a couple of shovels. We dug up sod grenades and began our sneak attack on the fort one foggy day. We forgot one important element of ground warfare, however. We forgot camouflage. The big kids spied us right away and laid down a line of fire with their BB guns. We bombarded them with our pieces of sod, but we were outmatched in size, weight, age, and armament. Our only recourse was retreat.

Jerry proved to be a good soldier. He was in the thick of it the battle and was struck by BBs several times. Those things really stung when they hit bare skin, but nobody cried. They raised a welt that took hours to go away and were worse then bee stings. We wore them like medals.

The Old Barn.

The Big Lot was home to an enormous old barn, and a tree house that, it seemed to us, reached to the sky. No one on Harrington Street could remember who built it, but it was there from the first day I ventured into the Big Lot; the day my family moved from Kansas City to the house at 32 Harrington. The tree house was where the big kids hung out. Little kids, like Jerry and me, were not welcome, unless we wanted to be targets of BB sharpshooters.

Jerry was the littlest of the little kids, and when he found out we were barred from the tree house, he suffered the crushing disappointment that comes to five year olds. In order to help him cope with the situation, I told him the big kids kept snakes up there, trained to keep all of us little kids out. Jerry's eyes grew wider when he heard this.

"Yes! " I embellished. "They're big. Big enough to squeeze you to death!"

His eyes grew even larger and his lower lip began to tremble. He didn't cry, but he immediately lost interest in the big kids' hangout. Jerry didn't care for snakes any more than he did heights. The snake story was obviously a lie, but it was one of the rites of passage that you told littler kids lies. After all, only a week earlier I had fallen for the same exact line.

To keep his mind off the imaginary reptiles, I told Jerry I had an idea. "We can build our own tree house."

Jerry pointed out there was only one tree on the lot, and it was in use. Logic, being what it is, I suggested we dig an underground fort. The moment I said it, I realized it would be a very large undertaking for us, but I planned to supervise while Jerry worked the shovel. That' what chains of command are for. Jerry didn't go for the idea at first, perhaps sensing his part in its realization, but eventually I was able to convince him it was a good idea.

"Now," I said, "all we need is a shovel." Jerry volunteered there was one at his house, so off we went to get it.

This was my first visit to the Garcia home at 87 Harrington Street.

"What's that noise?" I asked as we entered the front door.

"That's just Loretta," Jerry replied.

"Who's Loretta?" I asked, because she had a shrill voice and a strange way of speaking.

"Come on, I'll show you."

I followed Jerry through the house, memorizing every detail. As we passed the living room, I noticed a television set. Nobody else on the block had a TV. The only time I ever watched television was standing on the sidewalk in front of the appliance store window. After a few minutes, the owner would always come out and chase me away. In the back of my mind was the idea that only rich people had televisions in their homes. Rich or not, I was planning on spending a lot of time at my buddy Jerry's place.

Jerry pushed me on down the hall. We passed a bedroom, and I could hear guitar music being played inside, but not on the radio: a real person was playing a real guitar just behind the door. Not wanting to miss a thing, I peeked inside, and there was Cliff, Jerry's older brother, sitting on the bed strumming away. He didn't speak to us. He just glared back with a look that made it plain it was time for us to move on.

Jerry grabbed my arm and steered me down the hall towards the kitchen. He whispered to me we should not bother Cliff, or he would get mad and yell at us. Cliff and Jerry Garcia were nothing alike. Jerry was chunky and easy-going; Cliff was thin and edgy.

We hurried down the hall to the kitchen, pushing and shoving each other, giggling the way kids do. When we got to the kitchen, there was a woman standing at the stove. It was Jerry's grandmother, Tillie. She owned the house; a large two-story, white-clapboard with a side yard and a garage under the house. Tillie was tall and slim with gray hair, and nice-looking--- a dignified grandmother.

"Who's your friend?" she asked.

"This is John. He lives down the street. He's six."

They may have spoken more, but I wasn't listening, because right there in front of my eyes was the most amazing thing I had ever seen in my whole life. It was Loretta. She was a huge red and green parrot, and she was beautiful. The only time I'd seen a parrot was in the movies, but this was real life and it was Loretta who clinched it for me. From then on I would definitely be hanging out with Jerry.

"Hello!" Loretta shrieked.

"Hello!" I echoed.

Wow! She can talk! This kid really has some life here. I could have stayed in the kitchen all day, talking with Loretta, but Jerry pulled me out of there and we went to see his room.

At first Jerry's room seemed very dark and spooky. He kept the heavy drapes at the window drawn, and only a dim lamp glowed in the corner. To me, it seemed very creepy for a kid's room, and I was ready to get right out of there – until I saw the drawings. They were all over his walls, his drawings, and it was clear that although he was only five, he was hooked on strange creatures. His artwork turned the room into a monster's cave, which was obviously his intention.

After I recovered a little bit, Jerry showed me other drawings he had done. They were mostly comic book characters like Frankenstein and other monsters, but they were good for someone as young as he was and I was impressed. I told him some of them reminded me of ones I'd seen in comic books. He explained that's where he got his ideas.

"You want to see my comic book collection?"

Is the Pope Catholic?

Jerry Garcia's comic book collection was a huge surprise. Huge is the right word, because there were so many of them. He had been collecting them for quite awhile, he said. (He continued to collect a comic book a day for many years to come.) Tillie was very generous with her grandsons and indulged them with everything she could afford. Wow, so many comic books! I had never seen anything like it. At that moment, even if I hadn't realized it before, Jerry was the most incredible kid I had every known, even if he was only five.

After reading comic books in his room and watching some TV, we remembered why we were at his house, and headed out to the back yard in search of a shovel. We were walking back through the house with the shovel, when Jerry's grandmother stopped us. She pointed out that if we were going to dig, it would have to be in the morning, because it was dinnertime. She invited me to stay and have dinner with them, but I was expected at home, no exceptions.

At dinner that night my family heard all about Jerry Garcia, my friend who was a great artist, who owned a parrot, slept in a dark bedroom and who had the biggest and best comic book collection in the whole world. Throughout the entire dinner, I told them about my cool new friend.

They listened, because when you live on a one-block street, you know everyone's business, and they know yours. The neighborhood grapevine was fast, efficient, and designed to prevent small boys from having any fun at all, even when they were a part of it.

The next morning I was out the door and over to Jerry's house bright and early. I talked to Loretta for a while, and then Jerry and I grabbed the shovel. We marched over to the big lot and began digging our underground fort. We picked a spot not too far from the tree house and began shoveling dirt. We took turns with the shovel, because it seemed to me Jerry wasn't digging fast enough. Even then, it took three days for us to dig a hole about three feet deep.

After crawling in and out of our fort a few times, it dawned on us that perhaps what we had was not a fort at all, but just a hole in the ground. We needed to cover it to make it an underground fort. We decided on wooden planks. Even though the tree house was constructed of just the planks we needed, our young minds warned us the big boys wouldn't take kindly to that. Besides, there was still the issue of the snakes. Neither of us was willing to test the validity of that story. Desperate, I suggested we look inside the old barn for raw material.

The barn was old, large, and dilapidated. If our parents even thought we would venture inside the dangerously rickety structure, we'd get it for sure. So, naturally, it was a young boy's dream, even though it was dusty and full of spiders.

We began our exploration and Jerry found an old hay chute that ran from the loft to the floor. Our undeveloped attention spans lead us to climb the rickety ladder and spend the next few hours sliding down the chute. The search for a fort cover was forgotten as we climbed and slid, climbed and slid, adding a layer of dirt to ourselves each time. Finding the chute was an adventure, and it takes a lot of adventures to fill up a boy's day.

I really caught it when I got home and began shedding dust and dirt all over the house. A couple of spiders had crawled into my pockets, and I learned that day that my mother did not care for spiders, even a little bit. It was several days before I was allowed out of the house. At Jerry's house, they apparently had a different view of dirty little boys, and a more liberal view concerning the insect world.

Eventually, Jerry and I found the board we needed to cover our underground fort, and we spent several weeks improving and modifying our creation. We dug a tunnel entrance so we could slide into the fort. This eliminated having to move and restore the planks every time we entered or exited. It also allowed us to cover the planks with dirt, rocks, and dried grass. We had discovered camouflage at last. We even equipped it with a high-tech cardboard periscope fashioned from one of our cereal boxes, and used it to keep a watch out for any of the big kids. We considered ourselves pretty smart to think of all this stuff. We certainly weren't your average five and six year old boys, no sireee. The fort became our sanctuary to hide from the world. Jerry Garcia and John Clark in a hole in the ground, sharing secrets as only small boys can.

Our next-door neighbors' were Italian, and it seemed they were always giving my mother herbs from their garden, and sometimes-even one of the chickens they raised in their back yard. The sound of a rooster crowing in the morning, and of hens clucking during the day and announcing each egg laying. You may think of San Francisco as a great sophisticated metropolis, but in those days people raised chickens and rabbits and pigeons in their backyards.

Our neighbors were Carmen and Albert. They served me my first spaghetti with pesto, and it immediately became my favorite. I made sure my mother always got fresh pesto from then on.

Carmen and Albert had a hearing- and speech-impaired son, Albie. He lived downstairs, and in those days, he was referred to as a deaf mute. My only experience with such things sprang from a film, The Hunchback of Notre Dame, and, at first, Albie scared me. That changed after I got to know him. Albie couldn't speak, but he grunted, and his parents were able to translate and respond cheerfully. We didn't hit it off right away, but after a while I discovered Albie was really a dependable, warmhearted guy. He was bright, and he seemed to know what you needed before you did, and he was always there when you needed him. I learned from my friend Albie that impairments carry compensation. I learned a lot more from him, too.

The first time I took Jerry over to meet Albie, they hit it off immediately. From then on, Jerry always took some of his comic books over to show Albie. They were both great collectors. Albie became a big fan of Jerry's drawings and the scarier they were, the more he liked them.

From my window I could see the railroad that ran south from San Francisco. Today there's a freeway where the tracks used to be. Whenever I heard a train whistle back then, I would rush to the window, watch the train go by, and try to imagine where it had come from and where it was going. I would daydream about being on the train, bound for some faraway place. To this day, the sound of a train whistle brings me back to that simple boyhood dream.

From that summer of 1947 on, Jerry and I were the best of friends. We went everywhere together. As boys will be boys, we got in a lot of trouble together. We also walked to school together. We got in fights together. We went forward in life together. And we almost got ourselves killed together, a couple of times, too.

CHAPTER TWO

The first time our boyish enthusiasm almost got us killed was when we decided we lived in a perfect location to stage a soapbox derby. Harrington Street was on a hill, and Jerry and I thought it would be a pretty good idea to set up a soap box race. We scrounged up an orange crate for the hood, and nailed tin cans on the front for headlights. We used our roller skates for wheels. (They didn't used to come with shoes attached; they just clamped onto your street shoes.) We spent hours designing and building our monument to speed. Finally, it was done and ready for a test drive.

We attached a rope to the front axle, which was a piece of scrap lumber. The rope was the steering gear. Pull on one side, the racer turned that way. Pull on the other way, it turned the other way. Simple, scientific, and foolproof. We took our racer to the top of this hill. I climbed aboard; Jerry climbed on behind me. A couple of kids gave us a running push, and within a few seconds we were flying.

Halfway down the block, I realized we had forgotten something. We forgot to install brakes. We shot across busy Alemany Street, hit the center divider and were thrown out of our racer onto the street, where speeding cars swerved out of their way to avoid hitting two small boys tumbling ass over applecart. I got my first case of road rash, and Jerry did, too. For weeks, while the scabs on our arms and legs healed, we were back at the drawing board, designing and installing brakes on our racer, which survived the ordeal in better shape than we did. We finally got the brakes to work, and we became the soap box racer champions of Harrington Street. We remained so, even though we had started a trend, and nearly every kid on the block was building himself a soapbox racer.

Our search for speed also led us to the urban sport of sliding down grassy hills on cardboard. This happened one day after classes at Monroe Elementary, when Jerry and I went exploring on the vacant lot next to the school. The lot adjoined the auditorium where plays and meeting were held. That auditorium is where Jerry and I saw The Wizard of Oz.

We saw some kids sliding down the hill on flattened cardboard boxes. It looked like fun, so I asked one of the kids if I could try. I sat on the cardboard and away I went, but suddenly found myself rolling head over heels down the hill. I had slipped off the cardboard, propelled into the dirt by my own velocity, and ended up tumbling all the way to the bottom of the hill. After my accident, I didn't think Jerry would attempt a ride, but there he was, blasting down the hill, excited, shouting. He did a lot better job of staying on the cardboard than I had.

I tried again, and with a few pointers from Jerry, made it to the bottom right way. We stayed there for hours, sliding down the hill on cardboard sleds before starting a game of King of the Hill. The latter required a mound of dirt, which was there, and someone claiming to be king, who climbed to the top of it and made his pronouncement, usually with a Popeye-like display of biceps. The game had only one rule, and that was the job of everyone was to get the King of the Hill off the hill and become king yourself. It involved a great deal of pulling, tugging, tackling, jumping-on and shirt grabbing, all activities that spell fun to little boys. We played for hours at this dirty, rough-and-tumble game, because Jerry and I both agreed we'd rather be doing that than spending time at home.

When we eventually got to Jerry's house, we told Cliff about our adventure on the cardboard. We were surprised when Cliff informed us he knew all about cardboard-sliding, and that he and his friends had been doing it for a long time down on Mission Street, where the overpass crossed over Alemany.

Jerry and I decided to check it out. When we got there, we found pieces of cardboard that had been left behind by the big kids. We were old enough to realize they hadn't left them there for us, but what they didn't know wouldn't hurt them. We each climbed aboard a cardboard and were off down the hill. Once again, we hadn't thought things through, like the brakes on the racer. Speeding downhill, we assumed we would stop before getting to our old friend, Alemany Boulevard, the traffic-choked artery leading south from the city, which is what everyone called San Francisco in those days. They still call it that.

We rocketed down the hill as though we were on ice, and went sliding right into the street – without benefit of the cardboard, just sliding on our little butts. That hurt a lot, but at least we didn't get as scraped-up as much as we had on our brakeless racer. When we got home, we put ice on our backsides, figuring if it could help a headache, it could help other parts of your body.

The Bullies.

On our way home from school one day, Jerry and I were confronted by some big kids who demanded we hand over our money. We didn't have any and told them so.

"We spent our lunch money on lunch," I said, hoping the cold logic of that would diffuse the situation, but just the opposite happened.

They jumped on us, took off our shoes, tied the laces together and threw them over the electric power lines. There were lots of shoes on those wires, but most of them were old Keds that were worn out. It was a San Francisco custom, and all over town shoes dangled from the power lines of Pacific Gas and Electric. Maybe we were lucky that day, because there were also some pants up there.

Anyway, we walked home barefoot. When I got home, I learned how hard parents work to buy shoes for their family. When my mother found out my shoes were hanging on the power lines, she got really mad.

Every time we walked past the shoes, there were new ones, along with some pants from time to time. Then one day, it was all gone. We thought it was magic, but it was more likely the power company. People still tie old sneakers together and toss them over power lines in San Francisco to this day.

A Normal Family.

During the quiet times when we just sat and talked, Jerry always wished for the same thing – a normal family. We had that in common. As young as we were, we sensed that our families weren't like other families. Jerry had never really recovered from his father's death. His mother ran a bar in San Francisco, and pushed the responsibility of raising her sons off to her mother. Tillie did her best, but she worked long hours as Secretary-Treasurer of the Dry Cleaners and Laundry Worker's Union.

Jerry and Cliff Garcia were on their own a lot, and both of them missed their parents. As much as I liked watching television and talking to Loretta the parrot, I knew Jerry's house wasn't exactly a happy home. Cliff and Jerry fought a lot. So did my brother and I. One day my mother came home to find me hanging my brother out the window. He was turning blue by the time she arrived. I was trying to get even for him being a tattletale and squealing on everything Jerry and I did. He was two years younger than me; you know how that goes.

My stepfather was an alcoholic, and my mom hated that. With our two dysfunctional families, Jerry and I spent most of our free time together at his house, where we could avoid the real world by watching Howdy Doody, reading and rereading comic books, and having pretend conversations with Loretta. Jerry even tried to teach me how to draw, but I had neither the talent, nor the patience, to learn.

We treated each other as brothers, and together we found a sense of family we did not otherwise experience. Neither of us realized at the time what the future held for that chubby kid I met in my hidden spot at the Corner Drugstore. We did not know we would be lifelong friends, or that he would become one of the world's most loved guitar players and a cultural icon. The bond of our friendship had been forged in the empty lots and the secret hideaways of Harrington Street. It was an enduring bond that would see us through the wild world of rock and roll, outlaw biker gangs, and the strange and wild times of the sixties.

Before all that happened, there were more Harrington Street adventures. We were just beginning.

CHAPTER THREE

To avoid being at home, his or mine, Jerry and I decided to really explore some of the world that lay outside our block. We had seen the Indian Cave on San Bruno Mountain during some excursions, and it seemed to be calling to us on this particular day. It was about four miles away, which was quite a hike for two young kids. Along the way, we had to pass by the house where Jerry had lived with his father. Every time we walked by that house there were tears in Jerry's eyes. Every single time.

When we got to the mountain, the first thing we checked out was the frog pond, created by a small damn in a stream. If you saw the movie Bullit with Steve McQueen, there's a scene when he's chasing the bad guy's car in a mountain area, and the motorcycles goes down. That's about where we were, except back then there was no highway, only a lot of space for Jerry's and John's adventures.

We went after the frogs first, trying to catch them by hand. We didn't get many, and those we did catch, we released unharmed. From the frog pond, we had a great view of Indian Head Rock. To us, it was eerie-looking, and its history had been enhanced by stories we'd heard about the Indian profile the rock resembled. The stories said ghosts protected the rock so no white man (or boys) could ever loot the treasure reported to be buried nearby. The frog catching was an activity we used until we could gather enough courage to continue on.

We were well equipped for our expedition. Our little knapsacks held sand-wiches and cokes, and we counted on defending our lives by using the ultimate weapon of small boys – our Boy Scout knives. We were ready for anything, so we headed cross-country toward the rock. As we were climbing a hill, we thought we heard some noises and stayed very still until they passed. After a tough climb, we arrived at the entrance of the cave and peered into the darkness with no idea of what lie in wait for us.

We stood there and argued over which one of us would go inside first. Our chain of command had long since rusted away, and now we just argued. The results were about the same. Jerry took a hiking stick he had picked up along the way and began poking it into some holes. What happened next I wouldn't have believed had I not seen it with my own eyes, but Jerry's hair stood straight on end, just like in a cartoon. He dropped the stick and began backpedaling down the hill as fast as his little legs would carry him. I watched for a second as a large bat exited the hole Jerry had poked and flew out of the cave.

Running with my back to the cave, I caught up with Jerry half way down the hill. Those Indians had powers we didn't want to mess with.

The Quarry.

One of our other exploring places was the quarry. It was located right next to the Cow Palace. There's a bowling alley there now, but in those days it was a very large rock quarry. It was a good place to look for frogs and snakes, and a great place to do our bombing. We would take cherry bombs, which were also illegal then, tie them to rocks, then toss them into the water that filled the quarry. We'd shout, "Fire in the hole," toss our explosives and watch as the water shot up when they exploded.

On one particular visit, we had a lot of cherry bombs, and we were throwing them all over the place, recreating battle scenes from movies we'd seen. All of a sudden, we heard a loud noise that wasn't one of our explosives. We looked toward the top of the quarry where the noise had come from and saw rocks beginning to slide down toward us. We had started a real landslide. Before you could yell "Jackie Robinson," I was tearing out of there, and Jerry was right on my heels. We just barely made it as rocks and huge boulders came crashing down behind us.

It was a while before we ventured there again, and it was only by sheer luck that we managed to scramble to safety that day. If we hadn't, the history of rock and roll would be a couple of chapters shorter than it is.

Chinatown.

Jerry and I bought our cherry bombs in Chinatown. In the late forties, no city in America was as intriguing, or as mysterious, as San Francisco. Chinatown, especially, with its people, their singsong language, the strange and delightful smells, the weird stuff hanging in shop windows – it wasn't like another world, it was another world.

We would hitch a ride on the rattling old trolley cars, and when we reached downtown we'd jump off and begin looking for Chinatown. The first time we went there to buy cherry bombs, we gave our money to a man who promised to come back with our merchandise. Naturally, we never saw him again. We went into the store where we'd watched him go, but he had vanished. We figured he had probably gone into the underground city beneath Chinatown. Stories about such a place were told everywhere, and it turned out most of them were true. Beneath the surface of the tourist-clogged San Francisco Chinatown, there was another city, an exotic place that dealt in drugs, gambling, illegal sex-slaves, and many other things little boys didn't know about.

After our first venture, Jerry and I were smarter and told the guy we were holding on to our money until he handed over the cherry bombs. He was reluctant for fear of the police arresting him, but rather than lose a sale, he chanced it, and we got our cherry bombs. Out of respect for the dangerous service he had provided, we became regular customers and returned to him whenever we needed firecrackers or cherry bombs, which we favored because they made the most noise.

The Tunnel and the Church Yard.

Another place we liked to use our cherry bombs, and one that was more landslide resistant, was the pedestrian tunnel under Alemany Boulevard. Devils that we were, we would wait until we saw someone enter the tunnel before we began our bombardment. Doubtless, we frightened a lot of pedestrians, and in our inno-cence, were having too much fun to realize what a nasty thing it was we were doing. We went there often, however, and it wasn't long before word got out and we were discovered and apprehended by the police. There we were, in big trouble again. This time, we were certain we were headed for jail, do not pass Go. My mother picked us up. She was very upset. So was Tillie. Spankings replaced jail time.

Down the street from the Corner Drugstore was the Corpus Christi Church. Jerry and I would often go there just for the peace and quiet. After a while Jerry stopped going inside with me because he didn't care for the church, but I kept going, because I liked the statues. I thought they would jump to life at any moment.

The church had a school playground, where we would play baseball and basketball. We used the wall of the building as a backstop and pitched against each other. One afternoon, Jerry, who was still developing his swing, hit a ball up on the roof. It was the only ball we had, and I told him he had to climb up the pipe on the side of the building and retrieve it.

After his experience with the palm tree and the forces of gravity, Jerry was reluctant, but as it was our only ball, he had little choice. He shinnied up the pipe, climbed onto the roof and tossed the baseball down. The job was half completed, and now he had to face the problem of climbing back down. The church had installed chicken-wire barricades to prevent young adventurers like ourselves from climbing on the roof. They also provided some protection for the windows. During his descent, he became entangled in the chicken wire fence that protected the balcony of the building.

It was obvious his predicament was serious. He couldn't move, and the chicken wire was cutting into his fingers as he just hung suspended there, screaming at the top of his lungs. I felt sorry for him, but I had no clue as to how to help him. I shouted for him to stop yelling, and to let go of the chicken wire so he could reach the pipe. He didn't stop screaming, but eventually he did reach the pipe and the safety of the ground. I always wondered two things about that. The first was why no one came out of the building to help us. The second was what would have happened to him. It was a 15-foot drop, and if he had fallen, he would surely have hurt his hands and probably a lot more. Try dropping five times your height sometime. After that Jerry wanted to stick with basketball.

It was another small-boy incident that would have changed the fate of rock and roll.

Fruit Raids.

We heard the big kids from the street were making night raids on backyards about a mile away, and coming home every night with apples, oranges, and pears. After a bit of detective work, Jerry and I found out exactly where they were going and decided to get some riches of our own.

Waiting until everyone was asleep in our two houses, we sneaked out and met at the little lot. It was night and very dark. Nevertheless, off we went, using the pedestrian tunnel to cross Alemany. It was pitch dark inside, and our imaginations were in overdrive, so we ran like hell through the tunnel, all the way to the other side without looking back, because we knew, we absolutely knew, the headless horseman was in hot pursuit. We knew he couldn't come out of the tunnel, and we didn't consider the fact we'd have to cross through it again on the way home.

We walked through the quiet, dark neighborhood to Cayuga Street, where all the houses had fruit trees in their back yards. We stopped at the first house and crept around to the back yard, only to find a fence we'd have to climb to get to the fruit trees. I helped Jerry climb up and was pushing him toward the top of the fence when I heard a loud rip. Jerry's pants! His whole back seat was torn out, and in the light from the street lamp I was staring at Jerry's rear end, and on his shorts he had painted little monsters. I got the giggles and started to laugh and we ultimately returned from that raid empty handed. It would be a lot of years, but eventually Jerry's drawings would appear again on clothing.

McLaren Park.

The first time Jerry and I want to McLaren Park, it was for an Easter egg hunt. My folks drove us there, where we joined a couple of hundred other kids, running around searching for eggs. Whenever Jerry found one, he would put it in his basket. Within a minute or two, I would sneak it out of his basket and put it in mine. I don't know if he ever caught on, but he never said anything. I guess this story confirms the fact that kids can be meaner to kids than anyone else.

A few years later, we discovered the horse stables in McLaren Park. It was the first time we'd seen a real horse outside of a parade, except for a friend of the family who had a ranch near Brisbane. I asked one of the people at the park if we could get a closer look at the horses, but I could see from Jerry's expression, he didn't think that was a really great idea. We both were more than a little put off by the smell. In the movies, horses didn't smell, and this was a sad but educational experience for us.

As much as we were repelled back then, a couple of years later I would end up working at the stables in exchange for riding lessons. My job: shovel manure and hay. It was hard work, but I did it because I both enjoyed riding, and especially racing, the horses at a fast gallop, my hair blowing in the wind. It may have been this exhilaration that led me to motorcycle riding years later.

I was becoming a pretty good horseman, and could barely wait to get out of school and run over to the stables. Pretty soon I began cutting class to go riding instead. Jerry didn't continue his association with horses much after that, but at one time, he owned a couple and kept them at his place in Marin County. In the seventies, I saw a photo of Jerry on a camel in Egypt. The picture blurred before my eyes, as I remembered our horseback days – one more adventure we shared to escape our world of pain and sadness.

Jerry Sings.

The first song I ever heard Jerry Garcia sing was, "When the Red, Red Robin Comes Bob-Bob Bobbing Along." He sang it over and over again as we walked to grammar school. Eventually, I started singing with him as we walked, and we sang that and a lot of other songs all the time we were going to Monroe. I often remember thinking that I certainly hoped Jerry never thought about making singing his career, because his voice was lacking something. Man, he sure proved me wrong

The Fire Alarm.

The school fire alarm is ringing, and Jerry and I are running like bandits down the street.

It started out innocently enough. We dared my little brother, who constantly bugged us to pull the fire alarm at school so we could go home early. We found him jumping up, trying to reach the alarm, but he was too short. Apparently little kids are not supposed to report school fires. As a sort of joke, Jerry and I lifted him up and dared him to yank the alarm. We dropped him and ran for the door. The police found us hiding under Jerry's bed.

I wasn't able to sit for a week. Tillie grounded Jerry for that amount of time. I never checked to see if we had police records, although if we did, it would have raised our stature in the neighborhood.

The Grateful Dead.

For such a little kid, Jerry had a very active imagination. Late one night we both slipped out of our houses and met in the big lot. Jerry had come up with a plan for us to go over to the cemetery and dig up a corpse and see if we could bring it back to life. He proposed it as a contest. First one of us would try, and if he failed, the other would give it a shot. The closer we got to the cemetery, the worse the idea seemed to me. We were about a block away, when I was able to talk him out of it.

Years later, when I heard the name of Jerry's band was the Grateful Dead, I wondered if that episode from our childhood influenced Jerry when he came up with the name. I also kept thinking how grateful those dead people (and their relatives) were that we didn't dig them up that, or any other, night.

The Bakery.

When Jerry and I were about nine and ten years old, we needed money to finance some of our schemes. We walked into the local bakery and applied for jobs. The bakery was housed in an old remodeled garage. The entrance was narrow, dark, and spooky, especially to a couple of little boys, but there was a good bakery smell that led us on.

Inside there were large brick ovens, sacks of flour and sugar stacked around, and a lot of tables for prep work. At the back, near the ovens it was very hot. We thought of it as hell with fresh-baked bread and rolls. The owner listened to us, determined we were neighborhood boys and hired us to work for 15 cents an hour.

We began by sweeping floors and cleaning up, but soon graduated to twisting the braided loaves of bread that were popular then. We could barely reach the tables to work, but they found stools for us to stand on, and we tried to outdo each other kneading and braiding the dough. We competed to see who could twist the most loaves in an hour. In an effort to beat Jerry to the prep tables one day, I ran into one of them and was rewarded with a huge splinter in my chest. It hurt like the dickens, but we got it out, and I went right back to work.

Neither Tillie nor my parents were too happy about us working. We were covered with flour all the time and even ruined some of our clothes.

The boss was pretty good to us, and he even gave us presents sometimes. Once he gave me a pen and paper set and gave Jerry a little drum. It was like Christmas, and we rushed home to show our families. They liked Gino, our employer, so they let us keep working. They also figured out that every minute we were working we were staying out of trouble.

The boss also made sure we took some bakery goods home, and that was a big hit with our families. The bakery turned out French bread, pizza, and a lot of other kinds of bread and rolls. Jerry and I worked there Saturdays, because that was when they needed extra help to get the pizza dough ready for Sunday morning baking. We liked the work and the people, and we stayed on about six months, until the bakery moved to larger quarters in another neighborhood.

The Drum.

I liked the drum the baker gave Jerry. So much so, that I asked my mother if she'd buy me one. I'm sure she envisioned coming home after a hard day at work and having to listen to her kid banging on a drum. Her "No!" was not a surprise, but it didn't lessen my longing.

I went over to Jerry's and complained to him about it. Tillie overheard me explaining how much I wanted a drum and took immediate action.

"Come with me," she said, and we walked up the street to the Woolworth five and dime store and marched right to the back where the drums were displayed. I saw a drum I really liked. It was almost too quick to comprehend, but the sales lady took the drum from the shelf, handed it to Tillie and when we got outside,

Tillie handed it to me.

"What's this for?"

"It's for you, John," Tillie said.

"Gee, thanks!"

Jerry's grandmother had bought me a drum. That moved her way up in class in my eyes. I took the drum home to show my mother but the dream ended right there.

"Where did you get this?" she immediately wanted to know.

"Jerry's grandmother bought it for me," I explained.

She didn't believe me. She marched me right back down to the five and dime and asked the sales lady there if I bought the drum. It was a different sales lady, and she didn't know, so my mother handed the drum back to her, grabbed my hand and took me home and spanked me.

Before, during, and after the spanking, I tried to convince her that Tillie had purchased the drum and given it to me, but she would have none of it. The next day I went over to tell Tillie what had happened. She walked back over to my house with me and explained to my mother the facts of the case---- that she did buy the drum and she had given it to me. She believed Tillie that it was an up and up deal, but it was too late, because the drum was gone.

Mission Dolores.

Mission Dolores is the oldest structure in San Francisco. It was built in 1776 by Indian labor with Spanish missionaries as part of a network of churches built the length of California. As a school project, I had built a clay model of the mission. I considered it my best class project and greatest creation, and I had worked very hard on it for a long time. I was carrying it home from school to show my parents and, for some reason, Jerry thought we should take it to his house. In fact, he insisted. I refused, and he grabbed the model from me. We struggled with it, and just like a scene from a bad movie, we ending up dropping it on the sidewalk where it shattered into a gazillion pieces. My beautiful work – destroyed. This incident led to our first fight. Sure, we had wrestled and roughhoused before, but this time it was for real. We wrestled on the ground, and I tried to hit Jerry, but we were too evenly matched and I never landed a punch. That didn't faze me. I was crying and swinging away, really heartbroken, as we rolled in the shards of my greatest artistic creation.

I was devastated. I promised myself I would never speak to Jerry Garcia again – never! It turned out to be a great lesson in life. I can't remember how long it was until he apologized, but I forgave him. Friendship survives the worst arguments and the world goes on.

Demolition.

One day after school, Jerry and I arrived at Harrington Street and were surprised to see one of the houses was being torn down. It was an old house, three stories, and the contractors had begun the job, working from the top down. To a couple of adventurers like Jerry and me, our mission was simple and clear. In order to put it into action, we rounded up some of the other neighborhood kids and went over to the old house after the contractors had left for the day. Our objective, of course, was to aid them in accomplishing nothing less than the total and complete destruction of the house.

This must have been a really great idea, because some of the big kids had it, too, and were already at work when we arrived. Our unofficial, but willing-and-able demolition team now numbered about 20 young men.

The inside of the house was a mess. One kid had a steel pipe and was punching holes in the walls. I ran upstairs and reached to open a door when a kid's foot came crashing through it. I recognized it – it was Jerry's foot! The next door was mine, if I could find one that hadn't been demolished.

Naturally, our demolishing, along with our yelling and screaming, attracted some attention, and someone called the police. They arrived just as we were shoving an old bathtub out of an upstairs window. It landed with a loud explosion just in front of the first squad car, spraying debris over the hood and windshield. Whatever sympathy for the games and adventures of little boys the policemen may have had was gone when it appeared we were trying to demolish one of their cars. It also destroyed our defense that we were only trying to help the contractors with the demolition.

Jerry and I ended up together in the back seat of the same police cruiser. As we were pulling away, I glanced back and smiled at the three-story house that was now a one-story house.

"Two stories down, one to go," I whispered to Jerry. He grinned, and I could tell that as soon as we settled our business with the police, we'd regroup and take out the rest of the building.

Our parents had different ideas about that. Corporal punishment and grounding comprised the justice system of our childhood. By the time it was over, the contractors had finished their job. There was a lot of yelling and screaming when the mothers came to the police station. A lot of kids got pulled home by their ears, and the line heard most often was, "Wait until your father gets home, young man." Some of the big kids were on probation and went to juvenile court, or as we used to say, "jury."

Water Balloons.

Jerry and I were on the way to Woolworth's to buy some candy, when all of a sudden, he was struck by a water balloon and thoroughly soaked. We looked up to see where it came from and spotted the big kids, including Cliff, peeking over the edge of the roof. As we tried to see who was with him, another water balloon came flying toward us. We hightailed it across the street and sought the safety of a doorway from where we watched as the big kids gleefully bombed almost everyone who tried to enter the store.

While we vicariously enjoyed the show, we naturally began to wonder how they got up there. Our keen young eyes strained for a sign. Finally, their ordinance exhausted, we saw the big kids come out of a doorway and dash off down the street. We had to check things out. We ran across the street to that doorway and went in.

It was very dim when we entered, and even though we were scared, we kept going until we found some stairs at the back of the building. The problem was these stairs went down--- into a garage. We took them anyway. Inside the garage it was spooky, and within seconds, our fully developed imaginations convinced us this was a place where fierce, hungry, kid-eating monsters lived. We spotted another set of stairs and ran up them quickly, anxious to be away from the hungry monsters' lair.

We came out on the roof into the sunlight, safe because monsters hate sunlight. We looked around, and the view was worth all our fears. We could see forever, all around us. We could see all the way downtown! But we didn't get much of a chance to enjoy the view. Several people, angry with the big kids' water ballooning, called the cops, and by the time they arrived, Jerry and I were the only ones on the roof. We tried to tell them we weren't the guilty ones, but they only shook their heads and drove us to the station house and called our parents. You know what happened after that.

Stealing Cigarettes.

We weren't interested in being criminal or in stealing things, but Cliff and the big kids had ways of convincing us to steal cigarettes for them. Jack's, the local Italian deli, was our target of choice. We'd filch some packs, and the big kids would take them away from us. If Jack (and there was one) called the cops, the big kids did what the thugs in movies did – they made themselves scarce until the heat was off.

While they were smoking the cigarettes we'd stolen, they devoted much of their time thinking up other ways to get us to do other stuff for them. They were masters of coercion and threats, and we were little, so we usually figured it was best to go along with them, as long as the stakes didn't go higher than cigarettes.

I suppose our revenge was they would smoke the cigarettes and die sooner than we would, but we didn't know that then. Nobody did.

Trolley Cars.

How do little kids learn all the things they have to know in order to grow up and survive in an urban neighborhood? They learn from the big kids. One of the things we learned was how to ride the "cowcatcher" on the trolley cars. In case you don't know, the cow- catcher is a metal frame on the front of trains or streetcars designed to remove obstructions from the tracks. As we spent all our money on comic books and candy, we were usually short of funds for transportation, so we learned how to ride free anywhere in the city.

The technique required more courage than skill. You had to jump onto the cowcatcher while the trolley was moving. The streetcar trolleys didn't go very fast, but there were no hand holds on the cowcatcher, and if you fell, the street was pretty hard. That we could kill ourselves doing this never crossed our minds. What we did worry about was what our parents would say and do if we messed up our clothes. Kids are terrible at answering parents' questions. Both sides in these confrontations were aware of this.

Jerry and I decided we wanted to go to Colma one day. Colma is a town that's mostly cemeteries. Not only was Wyatt Earp buried in one of them, but Jerry had a fascination with cemeteries. Now Joe DiMaggio is buried there, too. We didn't make it to Wyatt's grave that day, because when we jumped onto the cowcatcher, we must have grabbed something wrong, because we received an electric jolt that knocked us right back off on the street. Our clothes were badly torn, and we were bruised and scraped and dirty.

But we didn't learn our lesson about hitching rides, because a few days later Cliff, Jerry, and I jumped onto the back of a pickup truck. We figured the pickup would get us there faster.

The driver figured he'd teach us a lesson. He sped up and raced down Silver Avenue, really moving. Then he turned left suddenly and executed this move on two wheels. We wanted to jump out, but the truck was going too fast, which meant that, want to or not, we were flipped out of the back onto the street. I landed on my feet, and I felt like I was running 90 miles an hour to keep from tumbling. I ran into a parked car. Cliff crashed into a wall of the Jewish old folks home, and Jerry went rolling and tumbling down a hill.

We regrouped and decided a trolley might be slower, but they were a hell of a lot safer. Maybe we didn't learn about things from the big kids as much as we thought. Maybe it was just plain old trial and error.

CHAPTER FOUR

It's not until after you grow up that you realize parents and kids don't live their lives on the same page at the same time. The lesson was brought home to me one day when, for no apparent reason, my mother decided Jerry was a bad influence on me. Simultaneously, as if it were written in the stars or something, Tillie arrived at the identical opinion in reverse.

These busy but determined women spent much of their time and energy trying to keep us away from each other, believing our friendship would wither and die. They forbid us from playing together. We couldn't go to the other's house, and they made it clear walking to and from school together was a violation of the Harrington Street Accords.

What they didn't know was that kids' friendships are almost indestructible and that efforts to end them are futile. The clash of wills over such things is furious, but the friendship of little boys, at least in the case of Jerry Garcia and John Clark, eventually wore them down. Before that happened, however, we rose to new creative heights in sneaking around and getting together. We were usually found out, and we were always in trouble and being punished for deeds. At one point, after it became harder and harder to fool them, we decided to run away from home together

Nobody understood us, boo-hoo. Everybody was determined to keep us apart. With the world consolidated against us, we skipped school and just hit the road. The road carried us up into the San Bruno Mountains. The seasonal fog blows in fast from the ocean, and it was upon us suddenly and completely. At first we couldn't see a hundred yards ahead, and a few minutes later, it was too foggy to walk. It was also cold, and we shivered as we slogged along, one foot in front of the other, for all intents and purposes blind in the forest. In my mind I had images of search parties finding our bones in some remote place in the wilderness.

To make matters worse, it was beginning to get dark. The white batting we tried to walk in would soon be black. Suddenly, something reached out and bit me. I froze and then realized it was a thorn. We backed out, but somehow we were in the middle of a patch of thorns. No matter which way we tried, we couldn't find our way out. Unable to see our hands in front of our faces, we gave up the idea of running away and turned our thoughts to surviving the briar patch we had stumbled into. Some long minutes passed as we made our way slowly along, and then – there! Ahead we saw lights. We ran toward them, and when we stopped and looked, we were in Brisbane.

Brisbane is a small town about six miles from San Francisco, and in those days there were still farms between the city and the airport. The lights we saw came from a farm- house, and we hiked toward it. When we got there, we walked up and knocked on the door. A nice lady opened it and gasped. We must have looked like creatures from a horror movie, but there was something in our voices she recognized — fear. She invited us in, listened to our story and then drove us back to Harrington Street in her pickup truck. She made us ride in the back.

The reception we got at home was what you'd expect. When our parents grilled us, our answers were the same, even though we didn't rehearse them. No, we relied on the common excuses boys of our age know better than multiplication tables.

And our parents always seemed to ask the same questions:

"Where'd you go?"

"Just out."

"What did you do?"

"Nothing."

And for that, the usual penalties apply.

Alcohol.

One way or another, children learn about the vices of life. Our introduction to alcohol began innocently enough. On the way home from junior high, Jerry and I stopped off at a neighbor's house, an Old Italian gentleman who lived two doors up the street from Jerry. The old man was quite proud of the wine he made in his cellar. (A lot of people made a little wine in those days.) He showed us his grape press and other paraphernalia, and when he wasn't looking, we began to sample his product. Both of us hated the taste of the stuff, but nether would admit it.

Junior high buddies, and we were celebrating our first drunk night together. We got silly and started giggling at everything the man said, and it didn't take the old man long to figure out what had happened. He showed us the door, and we made it home, where our respective reception committees sent us to bed. The room wouldn't stop spinning. I prayed for it to stop. What I should have prayed for was how I'd feel the next day. Jerry was so sick he stayed in bed and vowed never to drink again.

I was ready to sign that pledge.

Santa Cruz Mountains.

It was after our introduction to the evils of drink that Jerry invited me to go to the Santa Cruz Mountains with him and Tillie. I had never heard of them, so I asked him how far away they were. I wouldn't mind taking a good, long trip far away from home. It'd be an adventure, for sure.

"About 60 miles south," he said.

"Wow! Let me ask my mother."

I ran home to plead my case.

"Please, Mom. Please let me go. I'll be good. I promise."

She had her reasons, and to a grownup, they probably made sense.

"You know I don't like you hanging out with Jerry. You two always manage to get into some kind of trouble. I've heard your promises before. They don't seem to work where Jerry Garcia is concerned." She was adamant. Case close. The Santa Cruz Mountains were history.

Not quite.

I trudged back to Jerry's. "My mom won't let me go," I explained. Tillie overheard me and said she'd talk to my mother and try to convince her to let me go. I don't know what the two women talked about, but whatever it was, it worked, and a little bit later, we were on our way to the Santa Cruz Mountains, half a world away, at least.

We were headed for Lompico, a small town where Jerry's father and grand-mother had bought some property. The countryside that flashed by the car windows was a beautiful sight. The countryside was not something I saw very often.

We arrived in Lompico and drove to the house they owned. There was a sign at the entrance of the property that read, "CLIFFORD-GARCIA." Those were the last names of Jerry's father and grandmother. A two-story house nestled against the trees, and it was obvious the whole place was in need of exploring.

After we unloaded the car, Tillie showed us the room where Jerry and I would be staying, and we immediately changed into our swim suits. On the way down from San Francisco, Jerry had told me about the swimming hole. As we ran out, Tillie reminded us lunch would be in an hour. Although he had described it to me in the car, when I saw it I could barely believe my eyes. Before us was a huge swimming hole with a giant tree trunk on the edge and a strong rope hanging from a branch that reached out over the water. Amazing! This was something out of Tom Sawyer or Treasure Island.

We jumped into a big inner tube and paddled to the island the tree stood on. Jerry was singing-shouting, "Yo ho ho and a barrel of rum!" There was no doubt in my mind; we were heading for buried treasure inside the trunk of the tree. As we paddled, we had to be on lookout for pirates and for the giant who guarded the gold doubloons. The tube bumped against the tree trunk, and we climbed onto it. I was getting ready to jump in and test the water.

"Don't jump!" Jerry shouted.

"Why not?"

"The water... it's full of leeches!" We had just seen The African Queen, and our little minds were full of what they'd done to Humphrey Bogart. No matter how inviting the water looked, I didn't like the idea of anything black and slimy sucking my blood.

We spent an hour or so floating around, being careful not to let our hands or feet dangle in the water. Had I looked closer at Jerry's face, I would have gone swimming. I found out later he was getting even with me for telling him the tree house on Harrington Street was full of snakes. By the time I figured it out, Tillie was calling us to come in and have lunch. We abandoned our float and ran back to the house.

Tillie had made us the most perfect lunch in the whole world: tomato soup and peanut butter and jelly sandwiches. But our delight in the food waned when she insisted we had to take a nap after lunch. Nap? Naps were for babies. We were big boys! Sure. Anyway, she made us go upstairs to the bedroom we shared, where we looked out the window at a little piece of the world that still needed exploring. Our goofing off ended when Tillie came up and told us to settle down or there'd be no exploring later. I finally drifted off to sleep, thinking about the swimming hole, the rope swing, and the leeches.

"No! Leave me alone! No!" It was Jerry crying and yelling in his sleep. I knew about nightmares and went over to him and tried to wake him up, but he screamed for me to get away from him.

"Jerry! Jerry, calm down. You're just dreaming." I started to shake him to get him to wake up.

"The little people are here again!" he yelled. "The little people are here again."

What was that all about? I tried to convince him there was nobody there but us. Certainly, there were no little people around. Finally he began to wake up. I asked him what had scared him so much.

"You were screaming about little people with big eyes." He just stared at me for a long time. Then he shook his head and said he didn't know what I was talking about. He had blocked it all out. I told him it was just a nightmare, but he didn't want to talk about it. He was still shaken and scared, but as kids do, we soon forgot about it, and I never brought it up again.

Sutro Baths.

Another place Jerry loved to go to was the Sutro Baths at the beach, out at the end of Geary Street. The ruins are still there. It was an adventure, because there was all kinds of neat stuff there, including a museum. Back then the baths consisted of four swimming pools and a diving pool; three small pools that were heated and one large one that wasn't. The diving pool was at the top, and you had to walk up a lot of slimy stairs to get there. One day, Jerry and I started up the stairs. I went first. As I neared the top, I could hear a noise behind me. Jerry had slipped on the slimy stuff and was falling down the stairs, headed for the big pool. Splash! I rushed down the stairs and jumped in and grabbed Jerry, as he was going under for the second time. Some other people helped me to drag him out of the water.

Jerry had some nasty scrapes on his arm and legs but other than that he was OK. He didn't talk much on the way home. We were both thinking of how he could have been seriously hurt or worse. It was a while before we went back to Sutro Baths.

Fleishhacker Pool.

Fleishhacker pool was fed saltwater from the local ocean and it was the largest outdoor pool in the world. It was right next to the zoo, so after going to the pool, we could head over to see the animals. There was a diving board, too. The first time Jerry and I went there, I dove from the highest platform, but after what happened at Sutro, there was no way Jerry would go near the diving board.

A few times we went out there, we found some crabs at the beach. Naturally, we transported them to the pool and threw them over the fence into the pool. While we waited for the streetcar, we tried to estimate how many toes got nibbled. Once, they found a baby shark that had entered the pool through a filter pipe that connected to the ocean. Another time someone stepped on a body that was lying on the bottom. A body. No, there were no grief counselors in those days. Actually, it was pretty scary for a few days, and then we forgot all about it.

Despite our pranks and that dead body, Jerry and I had some good times there, and also at the roller skating rink that was down the hill from Sutros, next to Playland. It was a huge rink and sometimes we would go there at night.

One night I was out on the floor trying to impress some girls, which is what you do at age 12. I don't know how dazzling I was, but I was giving it my all when I took a spill and heard a rip. You guessed it. I tore the seat out of my pants. Jerry could not stop laughing. That kind of evened the score from the time he went over the fence to steal fruit, and I had not stopped laughing at him and his underwear.

Playland had a merry-go-round and a fun house with slides and a barrel that revolved and dumped you when you tried to run through it. But our favorite was the spinning disc. Jerry and I would race each other to get on, because whoever got in the middle had the best chance to be the last one on. We took turns winning, but it was always a struggle, because we would be shoving each other to try and get the sweet spot. It was only a matter of inches, but it meant victory and staying on the twirling disc longest. We would spend hours on the disc or in the barrel or climbing the stairs to take the slide down. Then we'd head for the merry-go-round and jump on and ride for free until the guy kicked us off.

Guitar Lessons.

I decided I wanted to learn to play the guitar. After extensive pleading (OK, begging) on my part, Cliff agreed to give me guitar lessons. I was a terrible pupil. Jerry was more interested in drawing far-out monsters, and I just couldn't get the hang of it. Cliff spent a lot of time trying to teach me a few chords, but without success. Later, when I learned that Jerry was becoming a master guitar player, I remembered our early lessons together. Obviously Cliff's work was not in vain after all, and the world can be glad for that.

We were the two Adventurers, moving through the world together, friends, pals, and buddies for life. We had a lot of fights, petty squabbles that were forgotten before lunch. Every little boy needs a friend to walk along the paths of childhood with him. Jerry and I had each other. It was quite enough for both of us. Listen, it didn't get any better than that, which is why, when he moved away, it was a huge shock to both of us.

It never occurred to Jerry Garcia or to John Clark that we wouldn't always live on the same block and be best friends. Not in our darkest arguments, not in our heart of hearts. Nor did we have the slightest hint we would ever be separated. But we were.

It happened in junior high, the summer after ninth grade. Jerry and Cliff moved out of Tillie's on Harrington Street and went to live with their mother in Menlo Park, a town on the San Francisco peninsula, nestled next to Palo Alto, home of Leland Stanford University. It might as well have been the moon.

I began to miss Jerry before the car was packed. I was afraid I would never see him again, and I knew in my young bones I would never find another friend like him. I missed his crazy sense of humor, his bizarre drawings, and his outrageous ideas. I doubted I would ever see him again.

As it turned out, we remained close, and saw each other frequently until the day he died in 1995. I remain in contact with Cliff to this day, and we reminisce about the old days and about how much some things have changed and how other things have not changed at all.

Monroe, our old grammar school is gone. The once big and beautiful brick building was demolished. Generations of children from the Excelsior district passed through those old doors. Cliff reminded me that their mother had gone to school there. It's funny that we miss it now, but when we went there, we nicknamed it the Monroe Prison. It is a universal folly that we can't see the value of things while they are still with us.

Enough reminiscing. I'm getting ahead of myself. Jerry and I saw a lot of each other, and I eventually introduced him to outlaw motorcycle gangs. But there was a period of transition for both of us. It lasted about three years when we only saw each other occasionally.

I was working on the docks as a longshoreman's helper, making about a hundred dollars a week. In 1957, at age 16, that seemed tantamount to getting rich. Well, if not, it was very good money for a kid. I bought a used '53 Harley 74' panhead. It was red. I loved it.

The longshoremen were hard as old oak and didn't take any crap from anyone. They had a strong union and commanded a lot of respect, but I remember some of the older guys who had worked down at the docks telling me that in the old days it was different. As they would say, "We remember when boats were made of wood, and the men were made of steel." I guess they thought that longshoremen used to be tougher. I couldn't imagine how they could have been, judging from the guys I worked with. I felt honored to be working with them and tried to emulate them as much as I could.

The Hearse.

One of my friends, John Bacaluppi, owned a '47 Pontiac hearse. I asked John if I could borrow it. When he wanted to know why, I told him I just want to show my friends this wild car. It was lined inside with felt, and everyone who'd ridden in the back of it was dead. That's how I got the idea.

John gave me the usual warnings, but he let me borrow it. I drove away and immediately called Jerry and Carl Renner who lived a couple of blocks away on San Juan and some others who went to Balboa High School with me and asked them if they wanted to play a practical joke at school. After I explained what it was, they all opted in.

I picked them up with the hearse, and we scrounged up a box that looked like a casket. We put it in the hearse, with a bloody fake hand hanging outside. We hit school at lunchtime, when everyone was outside. When John found out what we were doing, he wanted to go along.

We found some white smocks and gauze masks, obtained some guts and a sheep's penis from a local butcher with a sense of humor. When John pulled up in front of the school, there was a crowd. At first they didn't realize what was happening. It didn't take long. When the girls saw the guts and the blood, they started to scream. Then Carl began swinging the sheep penis at the girls. Accelerated screams. We dropped the "casket" on the lawn, jumped back in the hearse and peeled away, laughing. It was fun for a day, and the memories linger on.

My 1936 Chevy.

I also bought a pristine 1936 Chevy from my girlfriend's father. It had 10,000 miles on it. He was in the merchant marines, and always out to sea. It was classic, a true classic of a car. Cliff Garcia swung by one day and asked me if he could borrow it. He was a merchant marine by now and shipped out a lot. Jerry had gone into the army. I was a little hesitant, but finally agreed he could use if for the day, if he'd pick me up after work. Deal.

I got off work and stood on the corner for over an hour, worrying that something had happened to Cliff. When I saw my car come around the corner, I breathed a big sigh of relief -- until Cliff pulled up. The whole side of my car was caved in. "What happened" I asked Cliff?

"Some idiot ran a red light and hit me, he said. I wound up losing the car, and Cliff lost his license. What a loss. I remember that '36 Chevy better than I remember all of my girlfriends of that era. None of them were classic.

Clear Lake – 1963.

When Cliff returned from one of his trips, I asked him if he wanted to go to Clear Lake in my "new" '57 Ford convertible.

"There's a condition, Cliff."

"What's that John?"

"I do all the driving."

That squared away, we headed for Clear Lake in my new car, with Mickey, who later became my wife, and Sandy, her girlfriend. She rode in back with Cliff, with the top down the whole 120 miles.

Clear Lake was the largest fresh water lake in California. It's 27 miles long, and on one side is Mt. Konacti, an extinct volcano some believe may erupt again. Below Mt. Konacti is Soda Bay, where carbonated water rises from below. Old spa ruins remain there today.

I kept an eye on Cliff in the rear-view mirror. He was not exactly digging the wind, but what the heck; it was get even time for demolishing my '36 Chevy. It was a postcard day, and it got even better as we entered Napa Valley. We proceeded to Calistoga, which is at the north end of the valley. Calistoga then was unlike the way it is now, saturated with fancy restaurants and yuppie hangouts.

Past Calistoga, we began to climb Mt. St. Helena. Author Robert Lewis Stevenson had lived here in a cabin and wrote. As we passed where he had lived, I remembered the time Jerry and I were at Lompico, looking for buried treasure just like in Robert Lewis Stevenson's Treasure Island.

It was slow going over the mountain with all the boats being towed. There were few places for boaters to pull over and allow cars to pass. I zigzagged around them, but Mickey kept telling me to slow down. The look on Cliff's face wasn't all that happy either, but that was because he and Sandy were not getting along at all.

When we got to the cabin where we were going to stay, we unpacked the car and took everything inside. My friend Marty was already there. It was his boat we were going to use for water skiing. Mickey and Sandy wanted no part of that. They wanted to take my car and drive around the other side of the lake to see some friends while we skied. I had zero luck loaning out cars, so I said no to their request.

Anyway, Cliff and I went down to Marty's boat. I had brought along my 8-mm movie camera and began filming. Marty skied first, while I drove the boat and

Cliff operated the camera. The spray was dark green from all of the algae in the lake. I skied next. Cliff passed on skiing, but at least he was getting some sun. He was really pale. I figured all his time at sea must be on the polar route or something. I wonder whatever happened to those home movies.

When we got back to the cabin for lunch, my car was still parked in the same place, but when I went to get something, I noticed the seat had been moved.

"Mickey, did you drive the car?"

"No!"

I put my hand on the hood. It was hot from engine heat.

"I told you not to drive the car! Where did you go?"

She finally admitted that they had driven around the lake to see their friends. I let it slide, but that was an indicator of what was to come after we got married.

After that trip, Cliff and I began hanging around together. He was living back on Harrington Street. Jerry seemed to be moving all over the place with his mom.

CHAPTER FIVE

I discovered I loved motorcycles just about as much as I loved anything in life. I enjoyed riding my Harley around, and I became friends with a biker named Bob Kauffman.

Bob was the cool guy around school, our version of the Fonz. He had a brand-new, candy apple red Harley-74. The "74" meant it had a 74-cubic-inch engine. All the girls thought he was Mr. Studly, and he certainly fit the part. Bob was about six foot three, with long blonde hair that gave him a leonine look.

I used to ride my bike to school, park next to Bob, and try to look as cool as he did; jeans rolled up, hair slicked back, a pack of cigarettes rolled up in my shirt sleeve. Everything was just like Bob, but it didn't work for me. All of the girls still crowded around Bob. Was it the grease on my jeans? (My bike leaked a lot.) Was it his new bike? Or his leather jacket? Maybe it was the flapping noise I made whenever I walked, the result of a torn flap on the sole of my boot that I never got around to fixing.

Bob Roberts.

One day when I was hanging out in front of the school, a guy pulled up and parked next to me. He was short, muscular, and really looked like a bad dude. On the back of his Levi jacket, he had a patch, which read "Vampires MC." This was my introduction to Bob Roberts. He later became president of the Frisco Hells Angels. Bob was in charge of the Hell's Angels at Altamont during the Rolling Stones concert when a person was killed in 1969, an incident the media claimed was the catalyst that began the end of the whole peace-love movement.

When I saw Bob there in front of the school, I was a little nervous about speaking to him. I wanted to know what the "Vampires MC" was, so I swallowed and asked him about it. Surprise. He was very friendly and told me that it was a motorcycle club.

The patch also had the symbol, "1%" on it. I asked about that, too. It meant that it was an outlaw biker club, as recognized by the American Motorcycle Association. Bob told me that only 1% of bikers were outlaws, so they had a patch made up to show that they were proud that they weren't like the rest of the crowd.

He invited me to ride with him to a place called Jebbies. As we were riding along, I wondered to myself if I was doing the right thing. Where was this place? Who and what was I going to find there? Should I just make a turn and go home, or what?

When we got to Jebbies, there were dozens of Harleys parked in the street. Jebbies was located on Mission above 30th Street. Bob and I parked our bikes and headed for the front door. Right in front of me, there was someone with a patch that had the Hells Angel's flying death's head insignia on it. This was the first time I had ever seen a Hell's Angel, although I had heard of them.

I was getting nervous now, because there were quite a few Angels, along with some Wild Jokers, Mofos, Presidents, Vampires, and Slowmotions. All of the local motorcycle clubs were represented.

In 1957, the clubs were made up of a variety of guys of different ages, some married with kids, and many had regular jobs. The guys and girls got together to party and ride, and to help each other out if need be. The clubs gave the members a sense of belonging that many of them had never experienced before. The motorcycles were mostly the same Harley 74's that the cops used, except without all the extras. That way it was easier to outrun the heavier cop Harleys.

"Come on," said Bob and started inside. I had come this far so I followed him in. As I entered, I could not believe how small the place was and how many people were packed in. A man who looked to be in his 40s, tall, clean-shaven, and stopped me and I thought he looked like an off-duty cop.

"Check any weapons here," he said. Turned out he was the owner. He had been a cop in New York City, I found out later.

"What do you mean, turn in your weapons?" The dumb guy who asked that question was me,. Everyone turned at once to look at me.

"Are you packing any weapons? Guns, knives, chains? If you are, they need to be checked in here with me," he said.

"I don't have anything," I replied, wondering what kind of place this was. It reminded me of an old-time sheriff checking the six guns in a western town. I glanced behind the counter where he was stowing the checked weapons and couldn't believe my eyes. There were enough weapons there to start a couple of small wars. All kinds of motorcycle chains, guns, and knives were heaped up behind the counter.

I turned to enter, but there in front of me was the biggest person I had ever seen! Mr. Huge! And one bad looking dude. He seemed to take up all the space around and looked like a brick wall standing there. This was my first encounter with Filthy Phil.

That was 1958, and I remain close friends with Phil to this day. He's still that big.

I edged around him carefully and went on into Jebbies.

Everyone seemed to be friendly, and I was having a great time. Then someone announced that it was time to ride. As each person went out, they stopped to pick up their weapons from behind the counter. All those chains and guns and knives disappeared into jackets and vests like magic. By the time we started out on our bikes there was no sign of any weapons anywhere.

There were at least 75 bikes parked out front, and more at the service station across the street. I had never seen that many bikes all together before, and when they all fired up, the sound was deafening. It was exciting and scary at the same time. I was hooked on motorcycles, no doubt about that. The power of that moment remains with me still.

"Where are we going?" I asked Bob, as we started our bikes and added to the thunder.

"To the Pits."

I never heard of the Pits, but everything had been fun so far. I would ride with them and check out the Pits. I stayed close to Bob as we headed down Valencia Street toward the Golden Gate Bridge. We were really moving!

We went through the toll plaza, and the pace picked up even more. We were tire to tire, and I didn't dare let up on the throttle, as I knew I'd get my ass run over. It was a heart-pumping experience, roaring down the highway with 75or 80 bikes all moving flat out and flying, hair streaming, mamas hanging on for dear life, with the squares in their cars all staring as we passed.

The highway patrol joined us at the bridge and tried their best to stay with us. Our parade became even longer, and motorists were just about blown off the road. I could see the looks on their faces as we screamed past. I checked my rearview mirror and saw that some of the cars had pulled off the highway, figuring it was best to just stay out of the way. When we had gone about 15 miles, we turned off on a winding road that led to China Camp, a state park.

The guys never slowed down as the turns in the road became more treacherous. Our bikes were kicking up a lot of dust and debris from the side of the road. Man, it was hairy. The view was fantastic, with the San Francisco Bay on the right and lush meadow- land on the left. The meadows soon gave way to a steep drop-off, and it was as if we were suspended in air, traveling at breakneck speed.

All of a sudden, two bikes roared past me. It was Filthy Phil and Frank Moreno. They were racing each other with Frank's old lady on the back of his bike. I came around an especially sharp turn, and there was Frank sitting on his bike with the rear wheel hanging over the cliff. He was yelling something, but with all the engines roaring, it was impossible to hear what he said.

I pulled over with the rest of the guys to check out was going on. When I got there, I realized what Frank was yelling about. His old lady was no longer on the back of his bike. She had flipped off when his back wheel went over the edge of the cliff. It was a long, steep fall, and we all were sure she'd bought it. I was afraid to look down, afraid to see her mangled body at the bottom of the gully.

When I finally did look, figuring we had to bring her body back up, there was Frank's old lady lying spread eagle on an old dumped mattress. She had fallen down the cliff and landed on the only soft thing within miles. Sympathy and joy? Not quite.

Frank screamed, "Get your ass back up here and get on the bike. We're tired of waiting around for you!"

Sensitive guy. When she made it up the steep cliff, covered with dirt, scratched, and bruised, she didn't say anything. She just got back on the bike, and we took off again. Theresa was a tough chick; Frank's old lady had to be.

Just before we reached China Camp, we turned off at an old quarry. There were already some bikes racing on the track at the bottom. Some riders were challenged by the steep hill climb, and they handled their heavy Harleys like lightweight dirt bikes.

There were some women on their own bikes. One of them had the nickname, Dynamite, and she was. She could ride! I remember a friend of mine from the Frisco Angels saying, "Back in the old days the women were so tough, you didn't know whether to fight them or fuck them!" He also said he usually opted to forgo the fighting part.

Mofo Chuck, president of the Mofo MC, was on the hill climb, making it look easy. He was smoking a cigarette! When Bob Roberts went up, he took the hill like it was so much freeway. Papa Ralph (president of the Presidents MC, that became the Hell's Angel MC), was winning all the races at the dirt track. He could do anything on a bike. But Bob Roberts was the best overall.

The great riders made the impossible look easy. I decided to try the hill climb. When I was halfway up, the bike flipped on me, and we went sliding back down, rolling ass over applecart. I had a lot to learn. I recovered from the fall and was checking my bike over, when I heard gunshots.

At the bottom of the quarry several guys were shooting at boxes lined up against the rock wall. It was like a Fellini movie, with the roar of Harleys and the sharp reports of gunfire swirling around the quarry walls.

After awhile, it was time to go. When we got back out on the road, there were police cars waiting for us. It was always going to be like that. We were outlaws and some of the clubs had pretty bad reputations. This was before the Angels became famous, and the clubs were not that well known to most of the general public.

We were escorted all the way back to San Francisco by the highway patrol, and from there the city cops took over. They ran checks on all of us and wrote all the tickets they could, and guys who had warrants were taken to jail, their bikes impounded. One of the good things about the club was that when a bro got busted, the unbusted bailed him out.

When we finally got out of there, we headed for a bar called Mario's Huddle. It was around the corner from Harrington Street, where I still lived. We all parked our bikes along the street, lining both sides, and I could see that the cops were still with us. As we were getting ready to go inside, a bike came flying down the street, going like a bat out of hell. It was a beautiful bike, fully chopped with ape hangers. For the uninitiated, "ape hangers" are riser-handlebars. It was Deaf Mute Gordy. He spun a donut right in the middle of the street. This was my first look at a guy who would be a friend for many years. Gordy was featured in Hunter S. Thompson's book, the Hell's Angels. The cops let Gordy get away with that stunt. They were patient and knew if they waited, something was bound to happen.

Inside, Mario's was very dark. The jukebox was blaring the Platters,' "Smoke Gets in Your Eyes." I'll say it did, as the place was packed and loud and smoky. I moved toward the back, and as my eyes adjusted to the dark, I could see quite a few Hell's Angels there with some other tough-looking dudes. I stopped to talk to Gordy, not realizing he was a deaf mute. He could read lips though, and there was a guy there who knew sign language, so he helped me communicate with Gordy. Gordy was a really good guy, and we shot the breeze for an hour.

Walking out, I heard someone say, "Hey, punk." I turned to see who it was and came face to face with a dude called Crazy Rock of the Angels MC.

"Are you talking to me?"

"Yeah, punk. What are you gonna do about it?" I asked him what I had ever done to him. He sneered at me.

"You're a punk, that's all." As he said it, someone stepped between us. It was Papa Ralph. The Presidents were an outlaw biker club from Daly City, and Ralph saved my ass that night. Crazy Rock backed off after Ralph stepped between us. I thanked Ralph as we walked off toward our bikes. He explained that I really hadn't done anything. I thanked him again, and he invited me to come to the clubhouse for the next Presidents' meeting.

Wow! The president of an outlaw biker club is inviting me to one of their meetings himself!

"Hey, thanks man, where is the clubhouse?" Ralph gave me directions and said I was welcome if I wanted to come. I told him that I'd try to make it, as I cranked my bike up and headed around the corner towards home.

When I got home, I kept thinking about the invitation from Ralph and wondered what went on at the meetings. I had heard a lot of stories about outlaw clubs, and some of them were pretty wild. So far, everyone I knew in the clubs had been pretty cool, with the exception of Crazy Rock. I decided to call Bob Kauffman to see what he had to say about the idea.

I called Bob the next day and we talked about the Presidents. I told him that I had been invited to their meeting. I filled him in on what I knew about Ralph and the others I had ridden with that day. Bob had heard some of the same stories about outlaw MCs, including that they were all motorcycle thieves. He advised me not to go to the meeting. We talked for a while longer, and I asked Bob if he would take a look at my throttle cable. It didn't seem to be working properly. "Come on by the garage tomorrow, John. I'll take a look at it." He had a pretty good garage at his house and he worked on his own bike.

The next morning, I rode over to Bob's, and he decided that the throttle cable on my bike needed to be replaced. He had an extra one there, and he went ahead and did the work for me. I asked him if he wanted to go riding, but he couldn't, so I took off down the hill by myself. At the bottom of the hill, I let off the throttle, and the bike went full speed through a stop sign, barely missing a car. I managed to hang on and wondered what the problem was. It turned out that Bob had put the throttle cable on in reverse, so when I let off on it, it would open up. I walked back to Bob's and talked to him about it. "John, I told you I had to put it on in reverse," he said.

"I guess I figured that out when I got to the bottom of the hill." I laughed. Some mechanic, I thought. I said so long to Bob and told him I'd catch him on the weekend.

I decided to ride by Balboa High School and see if anyone was around. As I came to the school, I realized that I had left my watch at Bob's and made a U-turn to go back for it. As I was making the turn, the throttle cable snapped, and my foot slipped off the clutch. Suicide. I bolted over the curb and crashed into the side of a house. I landed in the grass and lay trying to regain focus. I heard a door open, and an old lady came out and started screaming. "Look at what you've done to my house!"

"Your house? Look at my bike!" I yelled back.

The handlebars were twisted and the damage to the house really didn't look that bad -- a small crack in the siding. I tried to get up, so that I could get away from that hysterical woman. Hoping that I hadn't broken any bones, I finally made it to my feet and lifted the bike off the grass. Twisted handlebars and all, I started the bike and rode away slowly, the woman's screams following me down the block.

When I got home, I got the third degree from my parents. They wanted to know why my new jeans were torn, and how I got all those scrapes and bruises. They'd learn what had happened soon enough through the neighborhood grapevine, so I told them about hitting the lady's house.

"Get rid of that motorcycle before you kill yourself!" They demanded. I refused. I was not going to sell my bike now, not when all of my friends rode.

"We are not going to allow you to endanger yourself and others, and besides you're hanging out with a bunch of bums!" My dad yelled back.

We argued, giving the neighbors a good earful, and without either side yielding an inch. The next morning, when I went to the garage, a tempered steel cable was locked around the front wheel of my bike. Fortunately, the padlock was not tempered steel, and I was able to cut it off, thinking there was no way they were going to stop me from being with my friends. I drove to Bob Kauffman's house to see if he could straighten out the front end of the bike.

Bob was standing out front watching me come up the hill. I must have looked pretty funny coming up the hill all crooked, with the handlebars pointing off to the west, Bob was laughing hysterically at my predicament. When he stopped, I told him what had happened, and he finally asked me if I was hurt.

"No. I tore some new jeans and suffered few scrapes and bruises. I damaged some lady's house, and my ears are still burning from the bawling out she gave me." That started him laughing again. When the second wave subsided, I asked him if my accident could have something to do with that "new throttle cable."

He checked. "Yeah, John. Looks like it got stuck. A little grease will fix it, then we'll try and straighten that front end out."

It took most of the day to do all that, but we got the bike back into running condition, meaning I could drive without looking like I was trying to go in two directions at once. When we were done, I asked Bob if he'd like to ride down to Jebbies with me on Sunday.

"Never been to Jebbies," he said, interested. "What do they do there?"

"Play pinball a while, then go riding." I told him about the quarry trip of the previous Sunday. He seemed anxious to go and said he would meet me at my house on Sunday. As we talked, I was hoping I still had a home to meet him at, after cutting that chain off and riding off against my parents' wishes.

CHAPTER SIX

There were a lot of gangs in San Francisco, but you didn't hear much about them in those days. The reason for that is probably because the violence level wasn't what it is these days. Make no mistake, there will always be gangs, and gangs will always fight each other. Sometimes there's a reason for the fighting and sometimes there isn't. My best example of how this works is a little episode I had with the White Shoe Gang. No, they weren't tennis players.

I met a girl at the sweet shop on Geneva Avenue. Her name was Kathy Rose. I asked her if she wanted to go for ride on my bike. She told me she'd never been on one and she thought they were dangerous. She also made it clear she thought all bikers were hoodlums.

"One way to find out," I said. "Take a ride."

The next thing I knew she was climbing on back of the bike. We headed toward the beach. I stopped by Kauffman's to see if he wanted to ride with us.

"Hey, Bob, we're headed for the beach. Do you want to come?"

"Sure" he said. "I'll get my jacket and my keys." After a couple of minutes, Bob began yelling. "Where the hell are my keys? They were right here a minute ago." He pointed to a table in the hallway. Then Bob saw Kathy holding the keys in her hand. "Gimme," he said, but Kathy ran out the door with them, and Bob charged after her. He chased her all the way to her house, about three blocks. Man, she was fast. When she got to her house, Bob caught up with her, and he was pissed. I thought he was going to hit her, but he didn't.

"Just give me the fucking keys." He said. She handed them over and we headed back to Bob's house.

"Sorry," I said. "Where did you pick up that chick?" I told him about the sweet shop on Geneva.

"That's where the White Shoe gang hangs out," he informed me. The White Shoes were white guys who wore white bucks. All of them were in high school or had just graduated. We weren't back at Bob's house more than 15 minutes, when we heard a loud noise outside. We ran to the window. There were about 15 White Shoes standing around. They had busted Bob's car window. My bike was safe in his garage. Bob's face turned beet red as he headed for the garage, me right behind. When we got to the garage, Bob grabbed his chain, and I grabbed mine. He opened the garage door and we came out swinging.

We hit a couple of them hard, and some of them brought out knives. Bob didn't blink. He went back in the garage, and he came out with a shotgun. The White Shoes scattered. I had never seen Bob so pissed. They didn't return that day, but we did have trouble with them over the years. As you probably figured out by now, Sweet Shop Kathy had called them. She was part of the gang, and she had set me up.

I headed home for a session of heavy begging and pleading, after which my parents allowed me to keep the bike.

"But no night riding, and no more hanging out with those bums." I agreed, but only to appease them, as I had no intention of allowing them to dictate who my friends were. Yeah, those kinds of battles went on even then. What? You thought your parents invented that problem? Ha!

Important historical fact: I still had my bike.

Mel's Drive -In.

Mel's was made famous when George Lucas featured it in his film, "American Graffiti." It was on the corner of Mission and Geneva, and the father of a good friend of mine, Steve Weiss, owned it. Steve and I double-dated one night and took our dates to Mel's. The girls didn't know Steve's father owned the place and stuffed silverware and salt shakers into their purses. We debated on whether to tell them, but figured it would ruin our chances with them later on. We laughed about that later, because we didn't have a chance with those girls anyway.

This was my first trip to Mel's on the bike. It took about two seconds to discover hot rodders didn't like bikers, even a little bit. There was no getting along with those guys when they were all together. When I pulled into Mel's, I could feel the cold stares. They really made me feel like an outcast, but then I figured that since I was an outcast, it didn't matter what they thought. I was actually proud of it. Who wants to be normal like the rest of the crowd? From the looks of the so-called normal people, I would much rather be an outcast.

I did like their cars. There were some really sharp '57 Chevies and '40 Fords. The place was packed, with everyone vying for the best parking places and the coolest chicks. I found a place to park and put the kickstand down. Someone immediately yelled out, "Hey, look, it's a grease ball on a grease wagon." I had to find the smartass. That wasn't hard, and when I did, I hit him with everything I had. Next thing I knew there were five guys hitting me and I went down. They started kicking me, and I figured I was a basket case, until I heard the sirens. They sounded sweet this time.

When the cops got there, everyone told them I had started it. The cops had me on my stomach, with my hands handcuffed behind me. The cuffs were too tight. The more I yelled, the tighter they cinched the cuffs, until one of the cops kicked my arms up even higher. That hurt, and I yelled even louder, but they just threw me into the paddy wagon.

By the time we got to the cop shop, the police were sick of my yelling. I called them a few choice names, too. Inside, I demanded my phone call. It was panic city when I realized I didn't know who the hell to call. If I called my parents,

I'd lose my bike for sure. I ended up calling Bob Kauffman, instead. I filled him in on what had happened, and he came down and bailed me out. We went back to Mel's to get my bike. I knew I had to go to court, but I decided to deal with that when the time came.

I thanked Bob for helping me out and headed to Jebbies's.

"We'll take care of those punks some day! That's not the first time they messed with a biker!" Bob said. I also told him about the episode with Crazy Rock, and how Papa Ralph had stepped between us, and that Ralph had invited me to the clubhouse for the next meeting. Bob did not say anything.

When Thursday came, I went to the meeting at the clubhouse. I wanted to find out what being a member of an outlaw MC was all about. When I pulled up at the clubhouse, I saw some of the coolest bikes in the San Francisco area parked there. There were panheads, knuckleheads, and some real classics. Every kind of bike known to man was there. Some looked like they belonged on a showroom floor and some looked like they belonged in a junkyard. The rest were somewhere in between.

I was nervous about entering the clubhouse. I had no clue if they were going to kill me, or just beat me up and take my bike, as Kauffman suggested. While all these crazy thoughts were swirling around in my head, the clubhouse door opened and out stepped Papa Ralph.

"John, come on inside." he said. He held the door open, and I went in. It was too late to change my mind now. Besides, I didn't want these guys to think I was chicken.

The clubhouse was a concrete bunker with several chairs scattered around. The furnishings were Salvation Army rejects -- a few couches and tables. Some rough-looking dudes lounged around. I was introduced to Grubby Chuck, Dirty Ernie, Howdy Doody, Pegleg Larry, and Joe Bolanja. Pegleg Larry really did have a peg leg. He'd had it painted gold, claiming the man with the golden arm had nothing on him.

All the guys were checking me out. I felt like a piece of meat at the butcher shop. Nevertheless, I found a seat toward the back, as Ralph called the meeting to order, just like he was the CEO of a big corporation. He introduced me to the room and called for the treasurer's report.

The treasurer was Dirty Ernie. There was some growling about his report. Someone shouted, "Hey, fuck that!" To my stunned surprise, the Sergeant-at-arms fined the guy 50 cents for swearing. I couldn't believe it! Fined for cussing at an outlaw biker's meeting! They were acting like regular upstanding citizens! I figured there was probably a lot of money in the treasury, especially with the swearing penalties, but Dirty Ernie's report revealed they were almost broke. Someone speculated old Ernie might have dipped into the treasury to pay for his new bike.

That argument might have been exciting, but suddenly the lights went out, and I was under a barrage of fists. I started to hit back, but it was so dark that I couldn't see who or what I was hitting. I began to think that maybe they were gonna kill me as I'd suspected. If that were the case, I was going to make sure they weren't going to find that easy. The lights came on as suddenly as they had gone off, and I could see the chairs all strewn around, and a few guys were laid out with them. I hurt all over and wondered what the hell was going on. Ralph called over to me.

"You want to stay, John? This is part of the initiation." Part of it?

I was still conscious, so why not stay and see what else they had up their sleeves. Each of these guys had survived an initiation, and if they could, so could I. I told Ralph that I wanted to stay.

Everyone stood up and the chairs were all put back in place. In turn, each man came to me and welcomed me to the club. To a man, every one of them said, "Welcome, bro." I had never had a feeling like that in my life, and certainly none since. There was a moment, a special moment, when I felt as if I had just joined a family unit that would last the rest of my life and would turn out to be much more important than my biological family ever could be.

After the meeting everyone wanted to ride. We decided to go to North Beach. I was asked to pack Grubby Chuck, since his bike broke down. I said okay, but when Chuck got on the bike with me, I knew how he had gotten his nickname: the guy had not had a bath in a very long time.

We headed toward the freeway in the dark, and ahead of me I could see streamers of sparks. I thought someone was dragging something and asked what it was. Chuck told me a lot of the guys had steel plates on their boots and dragged their feet to make those sparks. It looked like a fireworks display. People in cars had to wonder what was going to happen next. I wanted to get some plates on my boots for the next ride, but first I would have to get all the holes patched up so the plates would stay on.

We got to Market Street, and some guys rode down the crowded sidewalk. People scattered like bowling pins. It was something to ride into the hallway of the Emporium Store, and watch the window shoppers fly like leaves in the wind of our passing. We heard sirens, so we took off toward the hills of Twin Peaks and left any pursuit in the dust.

We had split up to throw the cops off, and we all met up again at North Beach to ride through Chinatown. I kind of hated to scare those Chinese people though, because I really liked Chinese food. I hoped no one would recognize me. I didn't want to get a plate of food in my lap the next time I came down there to eat.

After Chinatown, we went to the Italian side of Grant Avenue. Chinatown ends at Broadway and Grant Streets, a sort of demarcation line between

Chinatown and Little Italy. Only, in San Francisco, we call it North Beach. It doesn't actually have a beach, but there were lots of coffeehouses full of chicks dressed in far-out outfits. It was the only place I had ever seen girls wearing fishnet stockings who weren't hookers.

We parked our bikes and went into a crowded coffee shop. There was an outlaw biker club with a reputation as a bunch of bike thieves. Our club had an uneasy truce with them. It was obvious why they had their rep. They had absolutely no respect for anyone, especially women. They called all the chicks in the place every rude, insulting name in the book, and some that hadn't made it into the book. We didn't think that was very funny, but they were getting a real kick out of it. I was sick of their crap, but I wasn't about to start anything. There were more of them than us, but we would have no trouble mopping the floor with them, because Papa Ralph had a well-deserved reputation as a fighter.

We decided to blow that joint and go to Ott's drive-in for some food. We blasted back through North Beach, down Columbus, drawing stares from all directions. When we got to Ott's, the lot was full of hot rodders. This time no one shot his or her mouth off about grease balls. That was one thing about riding with these guys. We got respect.

We parked and were heading into the restaurant, just as five police cars pulled up and the cops jumped out and blocked our way. One of them spoke to us.

"You can't go in with your patches on. The owner doesn't allow colors in his restaurant."

Papa Ralph looked around and said, "Well, those hot rodders are allowed in with their colors on." Ralph was right; the rodders did have their patches on inside the restaurant. The cops held a brief conference and reluctantly stepped aside. Another victory for Ralph. No wonder he was the head of the Presidents; he really knew when to hold 'em and when to fold 'em. He should have been at the U.N.

The jukebox was playing a song by the Everly Brothers, "Wake Up Little Susie." We sat there, and no one seemed to want to serve us. Most people treated bikers like society outcasts – unless they needed help when they were being mugged or broke down on the road. The club had courtesy cards that they passed out to people they helped. The cards said, "You have just been helped by a Hell's Angel," or our club, the Presidents. People didn't realize the clubs operated with a code the rest of society would have been wise to adopt, at least in the late 50s. It was also like a family to me; everyone looked out for his brothers and helped them when they needed it. Whether it was bail or a meal or a place to stay, the brothers were always there for each other. Nobody understood this about bikers then.

We finally were served and had a good time, playing the jukebox and joking around. We simply ignored the rest of the people. If they didn't like us, they were so square that they didn't know what the world was all about anyway. When we left to ride through "the beach," as we called North Beach, we made a lot of noise, and all eyes were on us as we roared away from Otts's. The cops were still watching our every move, so we pushed it to the limit. We liked to give the cops something to do, so they wouldn't eat too many doughnuts or OD on coffee. If that's an attitude, so be it. We didn't hate the guys in blue; it was just a game.

We rolled over to a place called the "Beer Keg" on Columbus Avenue. A few Angels were already there, including Deaf Mute Gordy, Filthy Phil, and the twins, Ray and Roy, whom I hadn't seen in a while. I went over to shoot the breeze with them and we looked across the street and almost fell down laughing. Papa Ralph had ridden his bike right through the front door of Bimbo's 365 Club, a nightclub that catered parties for rich kids. We watched as Ralph came flying back out the door, his bike making a terrific racket. He squealed to a stop in front of us.

"Hey, anybody got a tie?" Like any one of us would have a tie. "The doorman says I can't come in unless I have a tie on." Someone from the Beer Keg offered Ralph a tie. He put it on over his denim vest and burned rubber back through the entrance of Bimbo's. A few minutes passed, and we heard police sirens, just as Ralph came smoking back out through the door, three big bouncers in pursuit. We all jumped on our bikes and took off after Ralph, his tie flying in the wind. For once in my life I heard laughter drown out the sound of motorcycle engines. I didn't know that was possible.

The cops kept after us, and it must have looked like a movie being shot with a line of bikes roaring down the street with the black and white cop cars giving chase. We hit the freeway and headed back to the clubhouse, when one of the bikes in front suddenly went down, skidded down the concrete, sparks flying-- – but not from steel-plated boots. The rider was skidding along behind his bike, and they were really moving. No way a guy could ever live through that.

We all pulled over when we could, and ran over to see how our fallen bro was. It was Wild Larry. He was skinned from head to toe, all down one side, like a dressed out deer, and bleeding badly. The police caught up with us, and we were busted. The cops were pissed and made us lie face down, lined up on the side of the highway, handcuffed. The damp, cold San Francisco fog swirled around us, as cars slowed down to have a look. We were worried about Larry and asked the cops to help him, but they ignored him completely. We soon heard sirens and hoped it was the ambulance, but it was just a paddy wagon.

"What about our buddy? He's hurt bad," someone yelled to the cops, but the police told him to shut up and threw us all into the paddy wagon. When we pulled away, Larry was still on the ground bleeding. He was in agony, but there was nothing we could do.

Nobody said much on the ride to the jail. We all were upset and angry at the way the cops had just left Larry on the road, lying there, and we didn't even know if they would help him after we were taken away. Man, we never abandoned one of our own. Papa Ralph was riding way out in front and hadn't seen Larry go down, so he hadn't stopped and therefore didn't get busted. He later bailed us all out.

Larry died of the wounds he sustained that day. We all felt that if the police had gotten him some help right away, he could have made it. Of course, there was no way to prove that. Back in the 60s, the long hairs and outlaws like us were looked on as a real threat, because we wanted change. We wanted to be able to do our own thing. That was when I decided I could never trust a cop again.

We held a memorial service for Larry. All the outlaw clubs came. The Mofos, the Hell's Angels, the Rattlers (a black biker club), and the Vampires. We all honored Larry. He would have been proud.

At the next meeting, I was made a "prospect" and given a bottom rocker, the bottom part of the club's patch, usually with the name of the city the club adopts. I was excited and liked the idea of belonging to the club, until I found out that to initiate my colors, everyone had to urinate on them. The stables where Jerry and I shoveled manure smelled sweet, compared to how I smelled when they were through initiating my colors.

You should also know that there was one thing you did not want to do at a party. You never wanted to "fallout," which is pass out. If you did, everyone urinated on you. I did my best to never fall out. I did not want Phil urinating on me. A few times when someone fell out, they ended up being tied to a chair with a gag in their mouth. Someone would throw a lighted book of matches on their lap. It was one way to find out how someone would react in a situation. I never quite figured out what it really proved, if anything.

On my way home that night, I stopped by Tillie's house.

Cliff had moved back there, and Jerry was visiting. He was interested in hearing all about the Presidents MC, so I invited him to come with me to the clubhouse for our next meeting.

"Is it safe? What do you do there?" Jerry asked. I remembered when I wondered the same thing and used the reply I was given then.

"Why don't you come and see for yourself, Jerry?"

We agreed to meet there at Cliff's again on the next Thursday. When Thursday arrived, Jerry climbed on the back of my bike, and we took off for the clubhouse. When we got there, I saw that there were many more bikes than usual and hoped they were not going to have anyone new tonight, as I didn't want Jerry to have to go through the "lights out" routine. I felt proud as I parked my bike, even though I only had the bottom rocker so far. I saw the twins and we walked over to talk to them. They were in the Hell's Angels's now, and I wondered what they were doing at our meeting.

"We're here to talk to your club," they said. I hoped it wasn't bad news, but didn't have a chance to ask them then. I introduced Jerry to them, and I could tell he was in shock to be shaking hands with an outlaw biker. I'm pretty sure the ride down was the first time he had been on a Harley, too. Jerry didn't say a word as we went into the clubhouse. Inside it was packed, and I saw some members of the Angels and other clubs there, too. But it was still a mystery why the other clubs were there. Bringing Jerry didn't seem like such a good idea, because there was a lot of tension, and all hell could break loose at any moment.

"Is it all right that I stay?" Jerry whispered to me.

"Sure. You've been invited," I told him, hoping it would calm him down and that it wasn't too big a lie.

"When the fuck is this meeting gonna start?" yelled Grubby Chuck. There's another half-buck for the treasury, I thought, trying to keep my mind off the uneasiness that hung in the air.

Dirty Ernie gave the treasurer's report and announced he was getting the hell out of California. Maybe too many members were questioning him about how he had been able to afford his new bike, but everyone seemed to be letting bygones be bygones, wishing him luck, some of them even saying they would miss him.

Ralph announced the Angels' representative, and Ray announced the Vallejo Angels were having a dance Saturday night, and we were all invited. We were to meet up with all the other clubs at the Silver Crest Donut Shop at 6:00 P.M. and ride to the dance together. This was for a show of solidarity among the clubs, he said. The Silver Crest was on Old Bayshore Drive and was owned by a fellow biker; a perfect meeting place.

Jerry was interested in the dance.

"Is it like the dances at school?" he wondered aloud to me. He was 17 and just as curious as ever.

"I really don't think so," I said, but Jerry was still very keen to go, if it would be like our dances at school. I told him I really didn't think it would be like that, but Jerry still wanted to go. Someone asked if we could bring non-members.

Ralph said, "OK." He paused, and added, "If they're good-looking chicks!"

I told Jerry he could be my date and wear a wig, but he didn't think I was very funny. The rest of the meeting was the usual, boring stuff. To get him back in a good mood, I told him on the after-meeting ride we'd be going to Playland. We both still loved the place where we used to go to watch Laughing Sal and ride the merry-go-round. It was near Skateland and Sutro's, two of our other old haunts.

When the meeting broke up, Jerry and I went outside, where I had a chance to talk to Chuck, the Mofos' president.

In case you think all bikers are stupid cretins, you would have been delighted to hear me ask Chuck a question that had been bothering me for some time. I asked him what Mofos meant. He yelled "Mother Fuckers!" I thought he was calling Jerry and me a bad name. Jerry thought so, too. We both broke out in a cold sweat. Chuck looked like he could knock a horse out, just like Mongo did in Blazing Saddles. We didn't want to start anything with him. He took off, laughing. We finally realized he was telling us the name of the club. We were relieved and more than a little embarrassed at how naive we were.

All the clubs were invited on the ride so there were many more bikes than usual – about 40– when we roared through Golden Gate Park. The park was very dark, and all the guys put their boots down, so the sparks were flying in the night. As usual the cops showed up and pulled us over. They told Ralph we were not to drag our feet, because it was creating a disturbance. Ralph agreed, just to get them off our back, but as soon as they were out of sight, our feet were right back dragging the ground again.

At Playland, we parked our bikes and headed for the merry-go-round. It was a beautiful night, no fog, which was unusual at Ocean Beach. We all jumped on the merry- go-round, as the squares took one look at us and jumped off when the merry-go-round stopped. The operator told us if we didn't get off he would call security. We didn't feel like getting into anything right then, so we headed for the boardwalk.

I asked Jerry if he was having a good time.

"Yeah, John, these guys are OK!" I was glad he thought so, though not too many people would agree. We were always getting hassled by the cops, who maintained we were rebels and criminals and ran us in every chance they got. I still believe we were just a bunch of guys who liked to ride and have fun. We didn't mess with anybody, unless they messed with us first. We didn't believe we were any different than straight society; we just had our own rules, without the bullshit that tainted everyone else's life. There were a lot of urban legends about us, but we believed in ourselves and in our brothers.

We strolled down the boardwalk, looking for fun and chicks. Some of the guys had weird ideas about how to pick up a chick, saying things like, "Hey cookie, not you, donut, your hole is too big." Or: "Your legs are like peanut butter easy to spread."

No wonder no one had any luck. It was really raunchy, and it didn't surprise me when no girls at Playland would even look at us, but most of the guys were dumbfounded as to why the girls gave them dirty looks.

After awhile, we decided to ride again, and headed our bikes for the highway, where the long straightaway that divided Playland from Ocean Beach made a perfect drag strip. There was a marked off quarter mile, and when we reached the first mark, it was off to the races. Guys were popping wheelies all over the place, and I decided it looked like I should get with the program. I told Jerry to hop off. I gave it full throttle and popped the clutch, yelling to Jerry to watch. The front wheel left the pavement, and I was riding on the rear wheel alone, screaming down the straightaway. "Nothing to it!" I felt like a million, a big smile on my face.

That was a moment when I felt like a real biker, standing on the back wheel. My fiasco at the hill climb was behind me. Everything felt good. The earth was in proper orbit, I was with my friends, the roar of the engines cracked into the sky . . . man, it was something.

And then the front wheel came down and everything went wrong. I found myself on the ground, and Jerry came rushing over to me. My bike was headed down the beach toward the ocean, bouncing over the dunes at full speed; a riderless Harley headed towards some mystical meeting with the deep, blue sea. The Pacific Ocean breakers pounded the beach, competing with the roar of motorcycles, as the moon sat high in the sky watching the whole thing.

Flashing lights a little ways down the road diverted my attention. The cops had set up a roadblock and were waiting for us. I got up fast and looked back where I'd last seen my bike, hoping it hadn't made it all the way to the ocean. There it was, flopped in the dunes a short distance away.

Filthy Phil and the twins, Ray and Roy, were still at the starting line, and rode up to see if we were OK. Phil went over and lifted my bike up -- few men could do that -- and wheeled it back toward us. I asked Jerry if he was all right.

"Yeah, I'm OK. How about you, John?" We both got to our feet. God, or the moon, or the mystic sea was watching over us that night. Neither of us had suffered a scratch.

As there was a police roadblock, we decided to head over the center divide, down over the dunes, and back towards Playland to avoid the cops. We saw what looked like another roadblock at the other end, so we cranked out over the dunes again. What a ride! Dune-buggying on a Harley 74! The adrenaline was pumping, and Jerry held onto me in a death grip as we hit the asphalt again, flew up Ortega Street to 19th Avenue and pulled over. Phil asked us if we wanted to hide out at his house. We agreed, thinking it would be best to get off the streets and avoid the cops who were on the prowl for us. Jerry wanted to go home. He'd had enough excitement for one night. It was on the way, and when I dropped Jerry off, I thought it would be the last time he'd ever want to go riding with me. I was wrong.

We were almost to Phil's, when we spotted a police car parked in front of his house. We turned around before they saw us.

"It looks like they've got our pads staked out," Phil said. "Can we go to your house, John?"

I could just see the looks on my parent's faces when I brought Phil in to meet them!

"No way! Out of the question, sorry." We couldn't go to the twins' house; the cops would probably be there, too. I suggested we go to my cousin's house.

"Ray can we hide out here for a little while?" I asked when we got there. Ray was cool and showed us where to hide our bikes. After I had told him what happened, and we added the information about the stakeouts. We went in the house, and when I got a chance, I asked Ray if he had a beer. Sure do, John. Phil's eyes lit up.

We found out later most of the guys had gotten away. The police went to the clubhouses and ran checks on all the bikes for warrants. Back then, they would take you to jail for an unpaid traffic ticket. The harassment put many guys way in the hole for fines and bail money. It was expensive to fight the system. That was one reason the clubs were started, to try and get a little respect and a little power.

We stayed all night at Ray's and split in the morning. Before I left, I asked Ray if he wanted to come to the clubhouse on Saturday, and he said yes.

When I got home, I intended to tiptoe into the house so my parents wouldn't know I'd been out all night, but they were waiting for me. Mom's voice was a thunderous demand.

"Where have you been all night?"

"I spent the night at Ray's," I said as nonchalantly as I could and acting cool about it. (Hey, it was the truth.) They were mad that I hadn't called to let them know, but after calling Ray and getting corroboration, they let me off with a stern lecture. Was it getting easier or were they getting used to this kind of thing? I didn't ask.

CHAPTER SEVEN

One morning Mofo Chuck, Filthy Phil and the twins asked me if I wanted to ride to Clear Lake with them.

"When?"

"Tomorrow morning. Early."

I was up before the sun and coasted my bike down the hill, so I wouldn't wake up my parents. The guys were waiting up on Mission, in front of Mario's. Off we rolled to Clear Lake, 120 miles away. It was a nice ride until we got to the entrance of Napa Valley, where we ran into a bone-chilling tulle fog. Man, it was cold! We stopped every so often to warm our hands on our engines. When we finally found a coffee shop open, we stopped and went in to get warm. The only ones among us who weren't cold were Phil and Chuck, who seemed to have anti-freeze in their veins instead of blood.

Chuck asked for coffee, and when the waitress started to pour it into the cup, he said, "No, pour it over my hands." That stuff was hot, and she looked at him with disbelief.

"Pour it over my hands," he repeated. She did, and you could see the steam come off of Chuck's hands, but he didn't flinch. The waitress thought he was nuts, and probably didn't give the rest of us the benefit of the doubt either. Can't say I blame her.

After that we headed out again. It was a little warmer now. The sun was up and began to melt off the fog. When we reached Clear Lake, we went right to the marina, which was the only one in the area that was open. Phil knew the owner, who liked bikers, mostly because Pete Page's family had a place on the lake. Pete was in the Presidents MC, then started the Daly City Hell's Angels, when the Presidents became Hell's Angels. We parked our bikes and started to go inside the (?), but Phil headed for, and the pier. We thought he was going for a swim but we had no interest in watching him. It would be like Shamu the whale if he went in naked and he'd probably scare the fish from the lake and the campers from the county.

Turns out Phil had other plans. We were having breakfast (beer), when we heard yelling outside. We ran out and there was a guy on the dock waving his arms and screaming his head off. Out on the lake, there was Phil in a boat. Guess whose boat. Phil was obviously having a blast, but at any minute I expected to hear police sirens. The way he was maneuvering the boat, it appeared he would capsize any minute. We started to yell to Phil to come back in, but he paid no attention, The owner of the bar came out, went down to the pier and tried to get his attention. Mofo, Ray and Roy thought we all should hide our bikes. We were about to do that, when we saw that Phil was heading back to the dock.

He docked the boat and got out. He turned to the boat owner, said something to him and the two of them walked back to the bar. We met Phil and asked him why he'd gone off like that.

"Because I wanted to," he said gruffly.

"What did you say to the owner of the boat?" I asked.

"I told his sad ass that if he called the cops, I'd come back and burn his boat and his dock."

The bar owner said he'd make it straight with the guy, and we settled down for a few more beers before heading for the campground.

We set up our tents and smoked a little pot. That made us hungry, so we headed off toward the restaurant. Before we got to the door, some hot rodders pulled in, but when they saw us, they decided to go somewhere else. I breathed a sigh of relief, because I did not feel like getting into anything. I just wanted to lie on the beach, swim a little and take it easy. All of a sudden Phil picked up Ray, and carried him to the edge of the water and threw him in the lake. He turned and started for me. I ran like hell. Roy went with me to the restaurant. We all ate and after that there were no more problems.

That night there was some serious drinking, but we all ended up crawling into our sleeping bags and snoring the night away.

When we headed out the next morning. I had a hangover. So did the others, so before we left, we went to the bar for "Eyeopeners:" beer with a little ketchup. After a couple, we packed our sleeping bags on our bikes, and headed for home. I was relieved; we didn't have any more hassles. The only thing that happened on the way home, was that I swallowed a bug . . . a very large one.

Marked Men.

The police knew all our hangouts. They could---and did ---make trouble for us whenever they wanted. It usually came down to whether or not they wanted to commit the manpower and resources to roust us. A lot of times, they simply didn't bother us if we were drinking beer and raising hell on some deserted beach.

One of the places we liked to have parties was Thornton Beach. Thornton Beach was near the Lincoln Golf Course, near the entrance to the bay, close to the Golden Gate Bridge. During daytime, you had to dodge golf balls when you cut across the course, but at night, that wasn't a hazard. We rode our bikes down the dirt trails, and it was tricky, but manageable, if you were anything of a rider at all. However, if we had to carry kegs of beer, it was a tough haul. When Phil rode with us, he'd carry the keg over his shoulder, like a sack of flour. Phil was as strong as an ox, and everyone knew it. So did Phil. One night he was carrying a keg down the beach, and he slipped and fell down the hill, head over heels, with the keg chasing him. At the bottom of the hill, Phil stood up, picked up the keg and put it on his shoulder like nothing had happened.

We built a huge bonfire, and convinced the cops they didn't want to fight their way through the sand to get to us. We had all kinds of food to put on the fire. There were oysters, provided by one of the guys who didn't offer to say where he got them; chickens, that one of the guys had liberated from a back yard, and a couple of ducks from Stow Lake in Golden Gate Park. We piled on roasting ears of corn, and who knows what else. Of course, there were chicks, and a couple of them were getting naked. No one complained about that. Hey, we were having a great time when someone announced that we were running out of beer. We took up a collection – about 50 dollars---and gave it to Phil and Mofo Chuck, who volunteered to replenish our fast-dwindling supply of brew.

I did not know how they were going to get that much beer on their bikes, but what the hell, they could do amazing things. The last of our beer ran out a while later, but still no sign of Phil or Chuck. The consensus was the cops had grabbed them. We waited and waited. All of a sudden, we saw Phil's bike coming over the cliff, holding a jug of wine in his hand. On his lap was a six-pack that went flying through the air as Phil's bike hit the sand. Phil landed, crushing the beer, but he did not drop the jug of wine. Mofo pulled up, shut off his engine and was up empty-handed.

"Hey, what happened to the rest of the beer?" All we saw for our 50 bucks was a crushed six-pack and one jug of cheap wine. It turned out Phil and Chuck had gone to the closest bar and drank most of the money. They only had enough left for the jug and six pack. Everyone was pissed, but what could we do? We did what anyone would have done. We drank the jug of wine and the crushed cans of beer and had a great time anyway.

The Dance.

On Saturday, I went to pick up Ray (my cousin). Jerry had seemed to change his mind. We went to the clubhouse first. There were some bikes out front and Mofo Chuck was there. As we pulled up, he yelled, "What's happening?" with his big grin and his ever-present foul-smelling cigar.

"Where we going first?"

"Mario's, to pick up some other guys. Then the Silver Crest to meet everyone."

At the Silver Crest Donut Shop, there were at least a hundred bikes, and some black guys from the Fillmore District. Their club was called the Rattlers, and I met their president, a guy called Cherokee.

When Ray saw all those bikes, he got a little nervous, but we talked about it and decided there was safety in numbers. We had some coffee, and sat around killing an hour or so, until everyone showed. Then it was time to ride.

Nothing equips you for the excitement when over a hundred Harleys start up, most with souped up engines and loud pipes. Ray was ready to roll, and we took off, the Angels leading, then our club, the Presidents, followed by the Gypsy Jokers, the Mofos, and the Rattlers. Bringing up the rear, of course, were the cops. They weren't about to let a group like this one out of their sight.

We rode toward the Bay Bridge, with tourists staring and taking pictures. Children were snatched off the street, and the straights were looking at us like we were the Huns, ready to rape and pillage. We rode on past them all. When we reached the bridge, the pace picked up. It was really something, crossing the bridge with all those bikes and our thundering roar echoing off the metal girders and exploding in the tunnel through Treasure Island. The weekenders in their cars were blown away.

At the toll plaza (at that time there were toll booths in both directions of the bridge) there were another 50 or so bikes waiting for us. The toll takers told us to pull over after we went through. There were highway patrol cars waiting for us, and the police told us we had to turn our patches around. I don't know why the cops were so set against our colors, but they were always telling us to take them off, or turn them around.

The police advised us they would take groups of 20 bikes the rest of the way to the dance. Many of the riders were against turning their patches around. I could hear a lot of grumbling in the pack, and for a few moments, tension was very high, and it looked like there might be trouble. But the leaders of each club told his guys to comply, and everyone did.

"Man! How often does something like that happen, John?"

"First for me," I said. "Most of the time the cops just write tickets or take us to jail."

We took off in groups of 20, escorted by the CHP. Not only was that a rare sight, we didn't even have to pay them. Never got around to thank them. There were hundreds of bikes at the Vallejo Angel's clubhouse. Ray whooped as we pulled up, a good block away. I wanted to make sure our guys were there, because the place was crawling with a lot of tough-looking cats. I saw Crazy Rock in the crowd, and took a deep breath. We headed inside, sticking close to Ralph. Our club had about 25 members there, but at that we were seriously outnumbered. There were Angels from everywhere there; San Francisco, Oakland, Sacramento, and San Bernardino (or as we said back then, Berdoo.) I wanted to have fun and show Ray a good time, but with someone like Crazy Rock around, you never knew what might go down.

We entered the clubhouse. It was like a men's locker room. There were a few women there, looking tougher than the guys. Ray seemed to be in a daze, what with all the smoke and noise. Mofo Chuck was dancing; Bob Roberts had a girl, too, a real beauty.

I nudged Ray.

"Let's see if we can find a couple of chicks." Ray just wanted to watch for a while, so I headed off by myself to check for chicks and found a girl to dance with, after getting turned down a few times. She was pretty, so I asked her if she would like to go riding sometime. We were talking and laughing, enjoying the music and making plans to see each other again, when there was a loud noise, and people began to make it for the door.

"What was that?" she asked.

"It sounded like a gunshot. I'll check it out."

When I got outside, Ralph was there with a crowd gathered nearby. I elbowed my way through and found a guy on the ground, his face covered with blood. Filthy Phil stood over him with a smoking gun.

"Phil?" I looked at him and he was as calm as ever.

"Dude pulled a gun, and was going to shoot one of the Angel's prospects," he said. The gun Phil was holding belonged to the guy on the ground. Phil hadn't shot the guy; he had just beaten him up and taken his gun away from him. The gun discharged when Phil grabbed it. Nobody knew who the guy was. He wasn't wearing any colors, but I knew the Angels would find out who he was, and make sure everyone else knew, so we could keep the guy from causing any more trouble in the future.

"OK, everybody, the show's over. Back inside, we'll take care of this." The Sergeant-at-arms of the Vallejo Angels herded everyone back inside. I ran into Ray, who was inside. He was nervous.

"What happened, John?" I didn't want to upset him more, so I said, "Nothing. Just a bike backfiring."

"Sure sounded like a gunshot to me." I shrugged and let it go. Unfortunately, those that had been at the scene were now telling everyone within hearing distance all the details, so Ray learned the real story, and some gory embellishments in a few minutes.

"John, let's go." Ray's imagination was obviously working overtime, and he wanted no more of the party at this point. I looked for the girl I'd danced with, but couldn't find her. The gunfire had probably frightened her off, so I agreed to split with Ray. We went over to Ralph to tell him we were leaving.

"Sure, John, see you later at the clubhouse," Ralph said. Ray and I got on my bike and took off. On our way out of the parking lot, we saw police cars at the edge of the road. I had no idea what they thought of the gunfire, or why they hadn't checked it out. They probably figured if we wanted to kill each other, fine by them.

Ray was quiet all the way back to his place. When we pulled up in front of his place, I asked him what he thought.

"Wow, it was something else!"

"I hope it didn't turn you off about bikers."

"Most of the guys seemed OK, but I don't know if it is something I'd want to do all the time." There had been a violent incident and Jerry was never into violence of any kind.

"Let me know if you want to go riding again," I offered, but I knew it would be awhile before he'd take me up on the offer. He never got over the idea that there was a possibility he could be shot riding around with me, he did not ask me to take him riding again.

Fort Funston.

Our next club ride was to an old WWII battery fort, on the cliff overlooking the ocean. Fort Funston was near Lake Merced. It had gun emplacements, to guard the California coast and the entrance to the Golden Gate Bridge against enemy ships in WWII. And the hills were honeycombed with tunnels, most of them damp and seeping. The floors were covered with a couple of inches of water and mud, so if you hit your brakes, you just started sliding. We charged into the tunnels on our bikes, and pretty soon it was a game of chicken, everyone flying up and down, crossing inches ahead or behind each other. The mud was flying; the roar of engines was explosive and the layers of mud building up on our bikes and ourselves. Man, we spent hours in the tunnels, playing our dangerous games, roaring and splashing until you guessed it – the cops showed up one night, and shut us down.

When we returned, there was a tall chain link fence around the place, a beefy lock on the gate. Shut out again.

Another place closed to us. It seemed every time we tried to have some fun, the police showed up to make sure we didn't. We weren't destroying property. The old tunnels were relics of WWII. They had no commercial use. They were dirty and rat-infested. They weren't near any residences, so we weren't disturbing anyone. It was against our code to mess with anyone, unless they messed with us. Of course, then we made sure they wouldn't do that again.

Mt. Tamalpais.

My next ride from Jebbie's was to the Mountain Home Inn, on Mt. Tamalpais, in Marin County, across the Golden Gate Bridge from San Francisco. This time, I had girl with me. Bob Roberts was packing one also. As usual, we hit the bridge, and the cops were on us like bees on honey. We kept going, and never let up. Let 'em catch our asses. We hit the curvy road leading up the mountain, and I could not believe how fast we were going. The turns were brutal. I had been over the mountain many times, but never this fast. Bob was leading. I didn't want to look like a wuss, so I kept pouring it on, several yards behind him.

Everything was cool, until I came around a turn and there was Bob Roberts sprawled on the ground, his old lady two feet from him.

"Coming through!" I yelled. I cleared them by inches and pulled over to help. "What the hell happened?"

"The old lady leaned the wrong way and my peg dug into the ground," he said. Bob righted his bike, his old lady climbed back on, and we gunned out for the Mountain Home Inn. It was the first time I'd been there. Below us lay the whole bay area. We dug the scenery for a while, and I finally had to tell Bob how lucky we'd been I hadn't run over him and his old lady. Bob didn't speak, but his eyes indicated it was lucky for me I hadn't run over them. I chewed over that a while and acknowledged he was sure as hell right about that.

On the way back down the hill, I lost my brakes. All I had was compression to slow down with, and then, when I got to the bottom of the mountain, Bob fixed my brakes. "Try brake fluid, John. It works," he said. Bob helped me a lot with my bike over the years. And he helped me with many other things over the years.

The Hell's Angels, and other motorcycle clubs, hadn't yet gained the notoriety they achieved in the mid-60s, but we had some bad press, because of a few bad apples. Wherever we went, someone wanted to fight, to prove how bad they were. It was just like the old Western gunfighters, trying to make a name for them. Most of the challengers wound up on the ground, bleeding. Despite winning the fights, it got tiring always having to prove yourself. In later years that were one of the reasons many guys got out of the club. They were some who were so well known and had lost so few fights, they were always being challenged, and they just got disgusted and tired of it. If someone in the club started something, it was a rule the rest of the club had to finish it.

John Clark's Photo Album

Cliff and Jerry Garcia on
Harrington St., 1948

Cliff and Jerry
Harrington St., 1953

Ray Hahn, Howdy
Doody, 1964

Jimmy Souza, vice president of Frisco Hells
Angels, and Bob Roberts, President of Hells
Angels on Grant Ave. in 60s

67

Frisco & Daly City at SF Beach, 1966

Filthy Phil, Run to LA, 1960

Filthy Phil, Run to Reno, 1960

Poster for Party Grateful Dead Played at, 1969

Police Station
After Fight in
Precita
ParkBob
Roberts, mid-
dle: Flash,
right

John Clark & Elvin Bishop

Author John Clark & Bob Weir, 1999

Group Shot at Papa Ralphs, 1994Top left: Bob Roberts,
John Clark, Vic. Bob Hall, Bob KaufmanBottom,
left: Pete Page, Papa Ralph, Ray Sharpe, Don Bradshaw

CHAPTER EIGHT

I wasn't exactly the recruiting type, but one day I asked Bob Kaufman if he would like to come to one of our meetings. He was a good candidate because he was a good rider and a tough guy in a fight. He also had one of the nicest bikes around town. The bike was the main reason he was reluctant. He'd heard all the clubs were full of bike thieves. But I kept after him, with juicy details about the cool runs we took, and some of the stunts the guys pulled. Finally, to shut me up, he gave in and agreed to come to a meeting with me.

We rode to the meeting together a few days later. It was obvious he was having second thoughts. When we got to the Clubhouse, he caught the attention of some guys out front, as he parked his beautiful, brand new, candy apple red '59 Harley FLH. This did not sit well with Bob, so before he left his bike, he put a massive chain around the front tire and locked it to a telephone pole. I laughed.

"Bob, when you come out your bike will still be there, but the telephone pole will be gone!" I tried to reassure him that no one would dare touch it in front of our clubhouse, but Bob wasn't going for it. He kept looking back at his bike to make sure it was OK. I knew none of our guys would mess with it, but I had no clue about any of the other clubs. Hell, word had it some of them even stole from each other – something nobody in our club did then.

When Bob Roberts was president of the San Francisco Hell's Angels, he would never allow anything like that. There was no drug use allowed, either. A little pot was acceptable, but if an Angel was caught using hard drugs, his colors were taken away on the spot.

Anyway, back to Bob and his bike. When we got inside, Papa Ralph assured Bob that his bike would be fine. This assurance calmed him down, but he still went outside, every now and then, to check on it. After Bob had met some of the guys, he relaxed and began to enjoy himself. He could see that we were not some kind of monsters; just regular guys, not unscrupulous thieves.

The meeting was going better than usual. We discovered we had some money in the treasury, even after Dirty Ernie left. That was a nice surprise that made everyone feel pretty good. Bob was as surprised as I'd been when someone got fined for swearing. Bob laughed his ass off when he heard that. I think he wanted to shout "Fuck!" a few times, to see if it were really true, but he didn't. That would have cost him 50 cents, and that would fill a bike's gas tank then.

Bob changed his mind about Ralph that night, and he seemed to enjoy himself, and it hadn't cost him a penny. There was no "lights out" routine that night. In fact, I had not seen one since they pulled it on me. It makes you wonder. Consistency wasn't our long suit.

After the meeting, we rode down to meet Filthy Phil, Mofo Chuck and some others at the Rinky Tink, a bar on Mission Street, near Mario's.

When we got there, I met a guy named Moose Heineke, a Mexican Irish Golden Gloves Boxer. Moose wasn't very tall, but he was well built and had a reputation as a bad dude who'd never lost a street fight. Moose and I became friends that night, and I told him he could ride with me when we got ready to take off, as he did not have a bike.

When we left, some other bikers joined up with us, including Joe Sousa, president of the Night Riders. His son, Jimmy, later became president of the San Francisco Hell's Angels. By the time we reached the freeway, there were about 20 bikes in the group. Riding loose and easy, there was Phil, riding in the freezing night in just a leopard skin vest. His hands had to be frozen to his ape hangers. By the way, Phil is the first person to use ape hangers, and he used chrome legs from dinette chairs. Phil was one amazing guy. He still is.

We were cruising along, when I became aware of something wet on my pants leg. At first I thought Moose had peed on my leg, but I discovered my gas tank was leaking. I thought the fumes could catch fire from the heat of the engine, so I pulled up beside Ralph and pointed to my gas tank. We were going too fast to be able to talk. We pulled off at the next exit. Ralph thought I was trying to tell him I needed gas, but when I told him about the leak, he went into the restroom of the gas station and came out with a bar of soap. He rubbed the soap over the hole in my tank, and it stopped the leak.

When we got back onto Highway 101, I asked Moose if he was digging the ride. He was having a great time, even though we had our usual highway patrol escort. When we left the freeway, the local cops picked us up. The police all wanted to be sure we didn't cause trouble in their town. When we stopped in Millbrae to eat, the cops stayed right with us.

We pulled into a drive-in that was full of hot rodders. The rodders didn't want to start anything with 20 bikers, and peeled out of there fast, their tires smoking. Moose took off for the bathroom, and I checked my gas tank. Sure enough it was leaking again, so I followed Moose. I was about to open the door, when I heard noise, thumping and groaning, inside. The door flew open and Moose walked out. Behind him, there was a guy on the floor, bleeding.

"Moose, what happened?" I couldn't believe he had already gotten in a fight; we had only been there two minutes!

"Guy called me a dumb spic," Moose growled. "So I took him in there and cold-cocked the S.O.B." The guy on the floor was the dumb one. Moose wasn't very tall, but he was built like a brick shithouse, and his punch was like a mule kick.

I got the soap and left the guy who was still out cold on the bathroom floor.

His friends would find him soon enough, and then there might be more trouble. I told Ralph about the fight, and Ralph just said "Shit!" and gave a whistle and a sign to saddle up and leave.

Phil wanted to know what was up, but Ralph just snapped, "Let's go!" and jumped on his bike, still chewing his burger. We all took off fast, with French fries and burgers trailing behind us. Moose couldn't understand what the big deal was. I explained we had to be careful, because the cops were always looking for any excuse to bust us. Had they known one of our guys had gotten in a fight, that would be all they'd need to keep us there for hours, checking everyone and running all our bikes through every check in the book.

When we pulled out, Ralph figured, we had better get back to our own turf, and we headed north toward San Francisco, instead of continuing south to San Jose. We were back in the city in no time and right back at Rinky Tink's.

The Pool Table.

We parked and most of us went inside; a few guys stayed outside to keep an eyeball on the bikes and a general lookout for trouble. Besides, the bar at Rinky Tink's wasn't very large, so all of us probably couldn't get in at the same time. It was inconvenient, but we only had a few places we could go, as bikers weren't universally welcome.

Rinky Tink's had one small pool table, and at that particular moment, it was occupied by a very drunk dude who could really shoot pool. We watched as he beat everyone there. Then Phil challenged him. The drunk took one look and didn't have the nerve to turn him down, so they played. Phil immediately began losing, big time. Naturally, this pissed Phil off, so he threw his pool stick at the drunk. Unsatisfied, Phil picked up the pool table and threw it out the door. It flew through the door, crossed the sidewalk, jumped off the curb and hit a city bus that happened to be passing on the street.

The cops screeched up, lights flashing, but when they saw how many bikers were there and the mood Phil was in, they huddled to map out their strategy. Rejoining us, they decided it was the pool table's fault for getting in the bus's way and cited the pool table for hit and run. Or maybe it was hit and stand, because it hadn't moved.

We all had a good laugh about Phil's temper. A couple of the cops were neighborhood guys, and they usually let us slide, as long as there were no dead bodies and we paid for all the damage. I was among those who laughed at Phil that night, but I also learned real respect for him. Besides, I never wanted to get on his bad side. If you were his friend, he would give you the shirt off his back, but you didn't want to get Phil mad when he was drinking. That was true of most bikers. If you broke down on the side of the road, someone who would go out of his way to help, or if you were trying to kick your bike over, and it was kicking right back, there would be someone who could find the trouble and stay with you until you got going again. Bikers knew they could count on each other. That was part of the code.

After the mess at Rinky Tink's was cleared up, Bob Kaufman and I rode Moose home. Bob went with me, because he remembered I had a run in with the Los Banditos whose turf was around Courtland Street where Moose lived. Before I became a member of the Presidents MC, some of the Los Banditos had tried to get my school jacket, because it was red, like their colors. One of them grabbed me, and I knocked him out. The other two took off.

On our way to Moose's house, we passed a bar called Cherokee's, and Moose wanted to stop.

"I need to score some reefer." I wasn't crazy about the idea; I didn't smoke myself. I had heard too much bad stuff about the effects and had seen some of them. Bob said it was OK to stop, but I didn't tell him what it was for.

We parked, even though there were no other bikes around. We went into the bar. Bob and I were the only white guys there. Moose was half Mexican. I made a trip to the john, and when I came out, there were 10 Los Banditos waiting for me. One of them was the guy I had knocked out when he tried to take my jacket.

"Hey, man, we want your patch!" one of them yelled. I looked around for Bob and caught sight of him by the bar. While I was deciding what move to make, a full beer bottle smashed against my head and all hell broke loose. Moose appeared out of nowhere, and Bob jumped into the middle of it. We were cleaning house right and left, when I heard Moose let out a yell of pain. There was a steel support pole in the center of the floor. Moose had swung at a guy, the guy ducked and Moose had hit the post with the full force of his most powerful punch. We heard the police sirens. The Los Banditos, who were still on their feet, ran for the back door and left five of their buddies sprawled on the barroom floor.

I went over to see if I could do anything for Moose. He was gray with pain. There was nothing to be done but wait for the cops. Our bikes were right out in front. The cops talked to the bartender first. He happened to be Moose's cousin and told them the Los Banditos had started the whole thing. They picked up the ones left on the floor, and took them away. After the cops decided to let us go, Bob helped me wash the blood off my head. It was obvious Moose needed medical attention, but he wouldn't let me take him to the hospital. He insisted on going home, and you didn't argue with Moose. I helped him into the house and called Ralph to fill him in.

"John, do you guys need some help? Hey, we'll meet you there at Moose's as soon as we can."

A half hour later, I heard the roar of Harleys and Ralph, Phil and some other club members pulled up in front of Moose's house. I filled them in on the details of the fight, and Ralph said "OK, let's go find the SOBs!" We looked around the Courtland Street area for about two hours, but those guys were in deep hiding; we never saw any sign of them.

We finally gave up and went to the clubhouse, where Ralph's old lady put a dressing on the cut on my head. I thanked Ralph for coming to our aid. He brushed it off with a curt "Hey, that's what bros are for, John."

Later I brought Moose to the clubhouse, and I thought if I could talk him into getting a bike, he would be a great asset to the club. He brought his brother, Gino, with him. Everyone liked them, but Moose did not want to get a bike so that plan failed. Ultimately, Gino did become a prospect for the Angels, but the Gypsy Jokers killed him in Golden Gate Park.

That act marked the beginning of the end for the Gypsy Jokers. The Angels eventually ran the Gypsy Jokers out of California. I was with Moose the day Gino was killed. Moose was never the same after that.

CHAPTER NINE

I don't want to give you the impression that all we did was ride around with an attitude and look for trouble. The truth is, trouble found us a lot, despite the fact bikers were mostly guys who hung together, rode together, and partied together. We appeared to be wild and free, when all we really were was just free, period. A lot of strait-laced people got the idea we were all thieves and malcontents. If you look back, the hippies, who were just coming on the scene around that time, broke through with all their peace and love crap, and were dubbed flower children. But they brought along dope and all kinds of drugs that you wouldn't believe.

Us? We were just a bunch of guys who rode bikes and pounded some beers. Were there bad bikers? Of course. Were there bad police? Of course. We were an easy target. We rode motorcycles and made a lot of noise. While the police were stopping us, hassling us, citing and arresting us, the unguarded urban neighborhoods of America got overrun by the sneaky, quiet dope trade. The cops were hassling Harleys, while the streets were being flooded with heroin.

Go figure.

The Drag Races.

The first time I went to the drags, it was with Joe Bolonja, Phil, the twins Ray and Roy, and Pete Romero. Joe was going to race; we were going to be spectators. The drag strip, located at a place called Half Moon Bay, was down the coast from San Francisco about 30 miles. The drive down the coast on old Highway 1 is a great ride. Great, except for one section called Devil's Slide. As the name implies, there are always slides there, so you had to watch for rocks on the road. In the 90s, the whole road at Devil's Slide gave way and crashed into the ocean, closing the coast highway for months.

We met at the clubhouse, and we were ready to roll. Ralph was on vacation in Boston. Joe, Pete, and myself had our old ladies with us. Phil, Ray, and Roy were going solo. It was a beautiful day to ride. Ray Sharpe lived in Pacifica. It was on the way, and we were going to stop at his place for coffee. We did not see any cops on the way to Pacifica. We got to Ray's, and there were a couple of other Angels there I didn't know. It turned out they were from Sacramento. We asked them if they wanted to go to the drags with us, but they said they were heading back to Sacramento in a few hours. We thanked Ray and headed down Highway 1 toward Half Moon Bay. We cruised past Devil's Slide and kicked it up after that.

It was a blast being on the coast road, with all of the curves, the wind blowing through your hair, the air tasting like salt. My old lady, Suzanne, loved it, but she was nervous about being so close to the steep cliffs.

We pulled into Half Moon Bay Airport, where the drags were being held.

There were quite a few bikes, and a hell of a lot of hot rodders. As we drove in, I saw a guy I knew, John Guisty. John's father, Punchy, had a '40 Ford with a Corvette V-8 engine in it. Punchy was a character. I stopped to say hello to John, who had come to race his black '57 Chevy with a blown 'Vette engine -- a stone beauty. I introduced everyone and then John introduced us to his old lady; she was stunning. Of course, Phil could not control his tongue. I felt we'd better get to the track, before Phil started something.

Joe won his class. It was a great day, with no cops hassling us and hot rodders too busy to bother us. John's old lady came and sat with us for a couple of races. Phil had a lot of hot dogs, and a lot more beer to wash them down. But he was cool and trouble-free.

When it was time to go, we were headed out the exit, and Phil did a wheelie right in front of the cops. That usually sets them off, but for some reason, the cops let it slide. They were allowing the hot rodders to do burnouts as they left, so we got to pop some wheelies. The world can be as civilized as it wants or needs to be. They also understood that the sooner everyone got on the road, the sooner they would become someone else's problem. We didn't have many days like that.

A week later Punchy asked me what happened at the drags. "What do you mean what happened?" I asked.

"John's old lady said you made a play for her."

"That's a lie. I had my old lady with me." This was news to Punchy.

"John thinks you tried to make a play for his old lady. He's going to marry her." Punchy acted as though he believed me, and I thought that was the end of it. I headed down Mission, and a black '57 chevy pulled alongside me. It was John. He yelled out his window, inviting me to his house the following Saturday. He said he was having a party. It was the first time John ever invited me to a party. All of his friends were hot rodders. The only one that I got along with was Marty Bunn, a nice dude who later shot himself in front of a bar, on Ocean Avenue. It was over a girl. At first, I thought there had to be something up. But maybe Punch had explained things to him. "Hey, sure, see you Saturday," I yelled back. Later, I told Joe about the party. "Watch your ass," he advised. "Hey, let's all go. He didn't say I couldn't bring someone." The motion was seconded and passed.

We all met at Joe's house in North Beach on Saturday. John Baculippi was there and wanted to come. His car was full, and there were five more carloads of guys, and then about 20 of us on our bikes. We set up a caravan and headed for John's house.

John Lived near City College. When we came to his house, we saw the garage door was open. "I'll check it out," I said and climbed off my bike. As I entered the garage, someone bounced a two-by-four off my head. I went down hard, and by the time I struck the garage floor, everyone was piling out of the cars, jumping off their bikes, and heading for the garage. By the time I got on my feet, our guys had wrecked John's garage, beat up 10 guys who were with John and completely wrecked John's car. For good measure, they went over the garage again, and when they finished, it was a total disaster. John would not be racing anytime soon.

The next time I saw Punchy he was not too happy, but he should have believed me, and his kid should never have tried to set me up.

Gypsy Jokers.

One day, Papa Ralph went over to the Gypsy Jokers clubhouse. He did not know the MC war had started. Chico answered the door and turned white when he saw Ralph standing there. Chico had a shotgun in his hands and handed it to Papa. Ralph looked at the shotgun and said, "What the fuck? I came here for parts, man."

Ralph stepped inside. There were Gypsy Jokers sleeping all over the floor. One of them woke up and saw Ralph standing there with a shotgun. He started to pray. Ralph said it again, "I am here for parts." He got his parts and left.

Bob Kaufman eventually became a member of the Presidents MC and was made treasurer. We then brought in Pete Page as a member. He was the guy who'd warned Bob about the Presidents being a bunch of thieves!

La Honda.

At our next meeting, we decided to ride to the Santa Cruz Mountains. I knew Jerry really loved that, so I called and asked him if he wanted to go with us.

"Sure, John, I'd like to go. But I think I'd just as soon drive up in a car, OK?"

"If that's what you want. Meet us at the clubhouse Sunday, and we'll leave from there about 10."

"See you then, bye," he said.

When I went to Bob Kaufman's house on Sunday, he was waxing his bike.

"Come on, Bob. It's shiny enough, we'll be late." He was always polishing that machine and continued to do so for another 10 minutes. Finally, we got going and just as we were pulling away, Pete Page rode up. Pete was going with us, and it was going to be his first ride with the club. Pete was mostly a hot rodder, but he had a fine bike. It was a panhead like mine, but chopped and customized to the max. It was painted a shade of deep purple and sparkled in the sunshine. I kept wishing my bike looked as good as his.

When we got to the clubhouse, bikes lined both sides of the road. Jerry was already there. I was glad he showed up, even if he was in a car with a friend of his.

"Hey Jer." I said, as I pulled up alongside his car. "Ready to have some fun?"

"Sure," he said. "As soon as I park, come on into the clubhouse."

Pete and Bob had already parked their bikes and were waiting for me. I introduced Pete to everyone, and Pete seemed to like that. After introductions, we entered the clubhouse and headed for the coffee and rolls. I told Pete, Jerry and Bob to help themselves, which they did. All I needed was a java fix.

Ralph announced we would be rolling in half an hour, as soon as the rest of the clubs arrived.

"Ralph, where we going?" I asked.

"A friend's place in La Honda," he said.

Hot damn! La Honda was in the Santa Cruz Mountains, where Jerry and I had gone with Tillie. Whether it was Fate or just the weatherman, when we reached the mountains, there was a morning mist, just like the first time we had seen the place. I checked my mirror. Jerry was behind us. I stayed towards the back of the pack to make sure Jerry hung in there, and Pete and Bob stayed with me.

We got a lot of stares, because I have to admit, it was quite a sight to see so many bikes going through the mist, like a dream. Maybe a bad dream to some people, but to us, it was more than a little magic. When we reached the summit, everyone pulled over.

Suddenly, there was Pegleg, Phil, and some other Angel's running back toward us carrying detour signs. They put the signs across the road and detoured all traffic down onto a dirt road that led God knows who where. Then they broke out the beer and started to party, right on the highway. It was really something to see the faces of the squares when they saw the detour signs and all of us on the road, but not one of them stopped to ask what was going on. They continued on down the dirt road -- not exactly what they had in mind when they started out for a nice Sunday drive.

The show we put on wasn't bad, either. A lot of beer appeared from somewhere. Some of the guys pretended they were having sex with their old ladies right on the highway. That bugged the eyes out of the motorists. It was unlike anything I ever saw. The road blocked, people out for a Sunday drive diverted down a dirt road, and a bunch of outlaw bikers having an orgy on the road.

When we first heard the sirens, we headed for our bikes. We left the detour signs in place to slow down the cops. We were off with a roar! This was getting even more exciting and our adrenaline was pumping madly. We moved very fast through some extremely tight turns. I looked to see if Jerry was keeping up. He was. It looked like his friend wanted to pass us and get out of this, but he didn't dare.

We reached our destination, a hillside home in La Honda, which was barely a wide spot in the road. One of the guys there turned out to be Ken Kesey. As expected, sirens followed us in and 10 squad cars pulled up. The cops started asking who put the detour signs up and who threw the beer cans all over the highway. They were really pissed, and as no one would talk, they decided to check all our bikes. What's new? After all this time, the cops still didn't understand that we all stuck together. No one would rat on any brother. Their frustration made us feel great!

We partied all day in La Honda. There was a lot of pot smoked, along with a few other things. This was the first time that I tried pot. La Honda, California, a bright sunny day, the cops running checks on licenses, the birds singing in the trees, my childhood chum Jerry Garcia and I remembering little-kid days, and my introduction to the weed.

I pretended to be cool, but I was really nervous; I heard a lot of bad news about pot. I asked Bob, Pete, and Jerry if they wanted to try it. Bob and Pete said no, but Jerry wanted to. What the hell, there was no chain of command now. We had built a fort together, and helped tear down a house, and learned to ride together. Why not share this experience together? So inhale we did.

What began as just a strange feeling soon turned into paranoia. Were all the other bikers' eyes on us, watching our every move, our every intake, swallow, pause, and slow-motion release? It felt as if they were. I retained enough presence to debate with myself whether or not I was going to be able to ride my bike. And in some dim, distant hall of my mind, I remembered the cops were still out there, lurking, waiting for me.

Jerry and I felt invisible. We were behind a tree, but it felt like we were invisible; no one could see us. I asked Jerry what he thought. He just giggled and offered a big, beaming smile. Right after that, the giggles stopped and a feeling of panic set in. What if I lost my mind? The pot was getting to Jerry, too. How'd I know that? He thought he could fly and wanted to try his wings. Jerry obviously thought he was one of his comic book heroes.

"You can't fly, Jerry."

"I can! You watch."

"Don't be crazy. Be quiet."

It didn't happen. Jerry started down the hill with his arms forward like superman.

"Up-up-and-away!" he yelled. I stood there waiting for him to lift off the ground. I was tempted to follow him, but a little voice told me to wait and see if he could fly first. Jerry stumbled, fell, and rolled down the hillside. I canceled my takeoff. I helped Jerry up and checked him out. Everyone's eyes were on us.

"He's OK. Just tripped over a rock." No one believed it, because they heard Jerry yelling, "Up-up-and-away!" They smiled and let it go. The atmosphere, aided by the great outdoors and the pot, was extremely mellow. You get one guess as to what contributed the most to the mellowness.

Jerry and I left to get something to eat. The world still hadn't returned to normal, and I hoped we were coming down from whatever the high was. I did not feel like spending the night in the woods, nor did Jerry. There were cops to deal with, remember. The last thing I needed was to get busted by the cops for being stoned. We both finally came down, but not before making complete fools of ourselves.

It was time to leave. We headed for the Pacific coast highway. We were going to return home a different way than we had come. It was still hot and the ocean breeze felt good going back up the coast. We rode two abreast, with Jerry bringing up the rear as before. Bob was riding alongside me, with Pete right behind us. When we stopped for gas, Jerry pulled up and said that he was going on home. I hoped he would make it home OK, and that the pot had worn off for him. I worried, because I was getting residual kicks, indicating some of it was still in my system.

When we started up again, the wind had picked up, and it was harder to control my bike, but no one let up. I was getting a little paranoid and I did not know if it was the pot, or because of the wind. Bikers need their wits about them when speeding along the coast highway, and the combination of the pot and the wind made it an edgy trip.

All of a sudden I heard a loud noise, and right in front of me, one of the bikes had blown a tire and plunged out of control. I swerved to avoid hitting the biker. In my rear-view, I saw him run off the road and his bike flying, end over end. Everyone came to a halt and rushed back to help. The unlucky biker turned out to be Grubby Chuck.

We had warned him about his tires plenty of times. He had listened, but at least Grubby landed in some sand and was not hurt too bad. His bike looked to be OK. It was pure luck. We got Grubby Chuck cleaned up and carried his bike up back to the highway, put it in the chase truck and headed home.

End of a pretty damn nice day.

Angels Camp.

I was really excited when I heard that we were going to Angel's Camp. It's in the Sierras, in Gold Country. Yeah, it's the site of Mark Twain's story about the jumping frogs. Every year the chamber of commerce has a jumping frog contest and thousands of people show up – including about 30 of us this year. We met at the clubhouse and headed out early in the morning.

We crossed the San Francisco-Oakland Bay Bridge and turned south towards Stockton. From there we headed toward the foothills and the town of Jackson. I had read a lot of stories about gold country, especially Jackson, and when we got there, it was just like I had envisioned it. In fact, it was almost like a movie set, right out of the old West. We headed for the Jackson Hotel, one of the action spots in town, with the cops trailing us like a posse. We parked our bikes amidst the usual stares and ignored them. The Jackson Hotel was authentic, which means it was like a saloon in the movies.

I half-expected to see John Wayne any minute, telling us we had to be out of town by sunset. The Duke didn't, but the sentiments were all around us. The cops, the people, the customers in the saloon -- everyone obviously didn't want our visit to be a long one. It wasn't.

We had a few drinks and then headed out towards Angel's Camp. This was great country to ride through, every turn a new revelation: hills, worked-out mines, and small towns that time seemed to have forgotten. We didn't see a lot of cops, but we knew they were around. Phil and Mofo rode with me. This was comforting, because I knew if anything happened, they'd protect me.

We didn't have any run-ins with John Law all the way to Angel's Camp. When we got there, Phil headed for the nearest bar. I wanted to look around the town, maybe find the frog-jumping contest. Nice idea, but what I saw was a helicopter overhead --- a police helicopter. As if on cue, cops began to appear out of nowhere. Obviously, they figured we were going to be trouble, but we were there just like tourists, looking the town over, planning on witnessing the frog-jumping contests. Well, I was not going to see any frog jumps this day.

The cops began busting some of our guys who had warrants. They told the rest of us we were not welcome. Man, what a bummer, and here they are again abusing our civil rights because they thought we might do something wrong. There was nothing that we could do. The town's citizens and the tourists didn't like our looks, either. What none of them ever understood was that this was the thing that made us tight with each other. If they were trying to separate us, break us up, stunts like this provided all the more reason for us to stick together.

On the ride back, I tucked in beside Mofo Chuck. I looked over and he was lighting a cigarette at 60 miles per hour. I tried, but could not do it. I tried it several times before we got to Stockton. It remains a stunt only Chuck could pull off.

When we got back home, we started a collection to get the bros out of jail that had been busted by the Frog Police.

CHAPTER TEN

My next adventure was going to the Rattlers' clubhouse. The Rattlers were a black outlaw club and their clubhouse was located in the Fillmore district. It's now called the Western Addition, but it remains primarily in the black section of San Francisco. I was more than a little nervous about going there, because we were all white, except for Moose, who was Mexican-Irish. Moose had been hanging out with us for some time, and he was thinking of buying a bike. I hoped he would, as I was tired of packing people. Also, Pete Romero had a black old lady, and was always going to the Fillmore area to visit her.

When we got to the Rattlers' clubhouse, there were about 15 bikes out front. There was also a smell of great barbecue coming from inside. A tall black guy came out and greeted us. Turns out its Cherokee, president of the club. I thought he was a real Indian!

There were 10 of us, and Cherokee invited us inside. I was impressed with their clubhouse. It had large couches on both sides of the narrow clubhouse walls. At the far end, there was a jukebox, and a kitchen, the source of the wonderful barbecue smell. We were all hungry. It turned out that the Rattlers had made the barbecue just for us. Ralph thanked them, and we all headed for the food.

It was somewhat strange being in a black clubhouse. I had never seen so many black people in one place at one time in my whole life. They all were friendly to us, with the exception of a couple guys, who made it obvious they did not like white people. Plus, they didn't like the fact Pete had a black girlfriend. So you could say we dug into the ribs in a quiet, but charged, atmosphere. That was destined to change.

We all got along great, thanks mainly to Cherokee. He was a great guy and possessed a knack for keeping things on an even keel. I hit it off with him immediately. He told me I was welcome at the Rattlers' clubhouse anytime, and so was everyone else.

Ralph extended the same visiting privileges to the Rattlers for our clubhouse. Later, this proved not to be such a good idea. Not because of us, mind you, but because there were white racists all around our neighborhood.

Whenever the Rattlers showed up at out clubhouse, someone called the cops and we were all harassed. We felt a kinship with the Rattlers, because we knew how it felt to be in the minority and the target of harassment. Probably because of the hassles, the Rattlers stopped coming to our clubhouse, deciding to remain on their own, familiar turf. However, I kept going to their clubhouse, as Cherokee always made me feel welcome.

Once Cherokee invited me to ride with them down to another black outlaw club. The other club was down in Niles, located in the southern part of the East Bay, and once home of an old-time movie studio where Charlie Chaplin made a few films. I went, only because I trusted Cherokee. I was going to be the one and only white guy. I trusted Cherokee would watch my back if anything went wrong.

When we got to the clubhouse, the number of the bikes lined up out front impressed me. Most of them were dressers, which the guys in my club would not have been caught dead on. In case you don't know, a dresser is a big bike with saddlebags, a windshield, and the works. Our bikes lacked these niceties. However, the number of bikes was impressive just the same. We parked and went inside.

The clubhouse was packed, and they were setting up a screen to show some kind of movie. This was different. I wondered what kind of movie they'd show and guessed a few X-rated titles as we walked to the bar. We got drinks and I stood next to Cherokee.

The lights went out, and the movie started. I could not believe my eyes! There was no XXXX-feature or porno shorts. The movie was of their drill team. Here was an outlaw biker club with a drill team. It took all I had to keep from laughing. One laugh and I would have been history. About 10 minutes into the movie, the screen was knocked over. It was probably an accident, but it ignited pure bedlam. Knives and chains suddenly appeared and flashed in the dimness. Cherokee stood protectively in front of me and told everyone that I was with him.

It was over quickly. Seems someone had grabbed someone else's old lady. Bingo: weapons alert. I was glad it was over. The whole thing had me in cold sweats. Thanks to Cherokee nothing happened to me. I could tell there were quite a few guys who didn't want me there. Still, it was amazing our club got along with this black outlaw club, but did not get along with other blacks. I figured it was because we all bikers had a kinship, and we were all outlaws according to society.

When we got back to the Rattlers' clubhouse, I decided to call it a night. I thanked Cherokee for his help and went on my way. I had survived once more.

The Chains – 1958.

One Saturday, Mofo, Chuck, and Pegleg Larry came by Jebbies ready for a ride. I went along. We crossed the Golden Gate Bridge and coasted into Sausalito, then a small town with a fishing fleet and houseboats along the main drag. Today there was an added attraction – real, live Beatniks. Beatniks, a term coined by local San Francisco Chronicle columnist, Herb Caen, was used to describe members of the Beat Generation of poets and others, and was new to me.

The first beatnik I saw was a woman with fishnet stockings, also a first. We tooled through the small downtown area, past the coffee shops and bars where the beats hung out. It had a very European feel. (Today, a one-bedroom house in Sausalito can set you back three-quarters of a million dollars.)

We were nearly through the town, when a car pulled up behind us and started blowing his horn at us. We were riding four abreast and simply ignored the guy.

We were doing the speed limit. The idiot leaning on his horn obviously wanted to go faster than that. What he did next was the dumbest thing I ever saw in my life. He bumped Chuck's bike.

Did he have a death wish, or was he certifiably crazy? It didn't make any difference.

Phil was really getting upset. He gave the guy the finger. The horn blowing persisted. Phil dropped back and got in back of the guy's car and I stayed out front. Larry got on his left side and Mofo drifted over to the right side of the jerk's car.

Out came the chains. We wore our chains around our waists, or around our necks, and, of course, their purpose was to secure our bikes when we parked. Uh-huh. We came out swinging, and when we finished, there was not a piece of glass left in the horn-blower's car. Also, there were no taillights, windshield, headlights, or windows. As we proceeded with our work, I saw the look of terror on the guy's face. He was panicked, and he probably shit his pants.

My eye caught sight of a highway patrol car on the overpass ahead. I yelled a warning, and we split up and headed for the hills – fast. I doubt very much if that guy ever bothered bikers again.

We headed for the coast highway. North or south from the bay area, this road sketches the coastal boundary of California from Oregon to Mexico. We rode it a lot. Not only was it a beautiful, exhilarating ride, there were fewer cops. From Sausalito, Mt. Tamalpais, called "the Sleeping Maiden" because the profile of the mountain resembles a reclining woman, loomed ahead of us. All we had to do was scoot out of Sausalito, take the cutoff to Mill Valley, and we'd be on Highway One. We stopped in Stinson Beach to fill up on gas, and then headed on up the coast.

We glided past the Bolinas turnoff and through Pt. Reyes. About a mile past town, Larry laid his bike down; that is, he had an accident. He landed on the gravel road, and ended up with some road rash, but he just shook it off. He was as tough as they come. We finally reached our destination, the Russian River. As we rode into Rio Nido, the police were waiting for us. They had one question for us.

"Where are you going and how long are you staying?"

"I thought this was a free country," I said to one of the cops.

"Shut to up or else. Let's see some licenses." They ran warrant checks; we were all clean. They wrote us up for anything they could find – broken taillights, head lights, mirrors, and wrote fines for equipment violations. It quickly became an extremely expensive encounter.

Before the cops went on their way, they reminded us that we were not welcome around those parts and suggested we leave immediately. As we drove off, Phil flipped them the famous bird. Knowing Phil, they got off easy.

We stopped at the first restaurant we could find outside the city limits. It was a little roadside stand, and when we got inside, one of the locals made a remark about Phil. He laid the guy out cold. The others got the message, and you could hear a pin drop in that joint. Still, it was obvious we had better get out of there before we had the cops on us again.

"This is all the cops needed to lock us up, Phil. Let's scram the fuck outta here." He agreed and we hit the road. I had a friend who lived in Cazadero, which was not far from where we were. We decided to go there to lay low for a while. I called Jerry to see if he was home. No answer. We found a place down by the river to hide until dark. We could hear the police sirens echoing in the hills, and we knew they were looking for us. They didn't find us.

In later years, many of us got busted and ended up in jail, myself included. My crime? Fireworks. Yeah, they were still illegal and I still got them from that guy in Chinatown. As busts go, it was extremely small change.

Anyway, this night we made it back to San Francisco without a police escort. This was very unusual, because the police spent a lot of time looking for us, not only for what happened at the river, but also they were still looking for the bikers who chained the car in Sausalito. However, we made it back without any stops by the cops. Luck was with us, it appeared, but luck has a way of turning, and it pulled a 180 on us.

When I got back to San Francisco and returned to the clubhouse, several patrol cars were in front of the building. They lined us up on the sidewalk, just as Ralph came out of the clubhouse. We asked the cops what was up. They told us some bikers had assaulted a car, and a witness identified the perpetrators as belonging to our club. Ralph told the cops it couldn't have been us.

"They were all at the clubhouse," he said. A couple of the non-biker neighbors backed him up. Most of the neighbors liked us, because we kept the block safe. The cops cut us loose and left. Ralph wanted to know the whole story. We told him exactly what had gone down, and he told us not to ever let it happen again. It never did – technically.

North Country.

Our next run was to be up north, a 100-mile jaunt. A century ride is a long way to go. We all met on Friday with our sleeping bags strapped to our bikes. I brought the one I still had from my old boy scout days. We headed north towards the redwoods. I had been to the redwoods once with my parents when I was a young kid. I could not remember much more than it was a beautiful place, but I was excited about the chance to return, glad it was a perfect day for a ride.

Some of the guys were doing stunts on their bikes that were absolutely unbelievable. They stood on their seats doing 80 miles an hour, as others popped wheelies, and did stunts beyond Evil Knievel's wildest dreams. It was a sight to see.

We made quite a few stops on the way for gas and to get some beer from the chase truck that followed us in case of any breakdowns. It also carried our beer, food, and weapons. It was a scorcher of a day, and the beer was going fast. I hoped we'd have enough to make it through the weekend. Phil was going through quite a bit of Jack Daniels. He liked the Jack back then, and still does to this day. After a pit stop, we were on the road once again, until we arrived at our destination, a campsite alongside the Eel River, surrounded by redwood trees hundreds of years old.

We worked together, and it did not take us long to set up our camp. A few minutes later, I heard echoing shouts of those having target practice. Being in the box canyon, the echoes were intensified. Other guys were practicing burnouts on their bikes. A burnout is when you hold your brake and apply full throttle to smoke your back tire. Meantime, several good arm wrestling matches got underway. You know what? It was just like being back at Boy Scout camp. Well, OK, we had guns and we were having a lot more fun.

I hoped that for once we would not attract the attention of the police. After all, we weren't hurting anyone. Surprisingly, the cops did leave us alone. It was great camping out with the bros, and like the big kids we were, we were all starting to get hungry. It's an unchanging fact of life how great hot dogs and beans can smell when you're outdoors. Chasing the food down with a nice cold brew, how much better could life get?

Judging from the growing chow line, I was not the only one who had worked up an appetite. Right behind me stood a guy who was at least a big as Phil, maybe bigger. I tried to make small talk with him but he just grunted.

"Who the hell are you?" he asked.

"The guy in front of you," I said. Big mistake. The next thing I knew I was picking myself up off the ground. Never try to be funny with someone who does not have a sense of humor.

As it began to grow dark, some of the guys wanted to go into town to find some women. Some had brought their women with them. Since Phil, Gordy, and I hadn't, we volunteered to go into town on a beer run. When we came to the nearest town, we were feeling no pain. That's what two six packs of Country Club will do for you. The town had two bars and a gas station, period. It also had two cop cars that seemed to have our names written on them. I had this ominous feeling that once again all hell was about to break loose. However, feeling no pain, my numbed brain discarded the thought of any serious encounter.

About this time Phil hollered out, "Let them try to fuck with us!" We were to look back on that remark later to see that he was just priming the pump.

We pulled up to the first bar to park our bikes. There were a couple of guys doing burnouts in the parking lot and drawing attention to us all. At least the cops were holding back. When I got inside, I noticed a full bar. This had to be the towns only hang out. The bar was full of locals, plus a bunch of guys who could have passed for lumberjacks. We made up the biker contingent, and there you have a small, crowded bar compressed with three groups of what could be called adversaries. Dynamite with a short fuse.

I went up to the bar to get a drink, and from somewhere behind me, I clearly heard something often spoken when we bikers stepped into new territory.

"We don't want trash around here!" yelled one of the biggest lumberjack-looking guys.

"You guys don't look so tough!" another voice called out.

Phil laid that guy out cold. Then the combustible mixture exploded all to hell and back with pool sticks, cue balls, and chairs hurling through the air. Most found their mark. Zonk! My involvement was swift, as a cue stick crashed into the back of my head. It was the first time I ever saw stars, like the animated ones in cartoons. No cartoon here, though. It looked like we were doing most of the ass kicking, as there were more of their Asses lying still on the ground than ours. Our apparent victory was not to be, as the cops burst through the doors in force. Their clubs were flying and hitting anything still moving. As we were the main bodies still moving, we became the cops' main targets. Ralph laid out one of the cops, and Phil laid out another. Phil thrived on this type of excitement and looked as though he was having himself a blast, but in a few minutes they began to overpower us.

A few of us made it out the back door and split on our bikes, heading back for camp. When we got there, the cops had the front entrance staked out, and were waiting for us. Plan B. We tooled around to the back entrance, but they had that covered too. All I could think of was how I was going to lose my Boy Scout tent and sleeping bag, but I had no choice. We headed back to San Francisco and stayed on back roads as much as possible.

When I got home, it didn't take my parents long to discover I no longer owned any camping gear. After they hit the roof, they came up with an either/or ultimatum. I could sell my bike, or I could move out of the house. No way I could sell my bike, so I packed up and left home and was out on my own. I had a friend whose father was the controller for the City of San Francisco (later convicted of embezzlement) who owned two apartments. He let me have one of them. Mine was on Monterey Boulevard. It was three blocks from the clubhouse, near where Bob Roberts lives today. I was 18 years old, living on my own and an outlaw biker. Some resume.

In 1958, members of their respective clubs felt they had joined an ultimate brotherhood. It was pure family. Most of the guys who joined the clubs really did not have much of a family to begin with. They lived in a world with limited options open to them. When they joined a biker club, they felt part of a family that cared and would stand beside them no matter what. They felt respected, and most important of all, they were no longer alone. This allowed them to believe they had power over their lives. Maybe it was an illusion, but it was something. The worldly goods of most of the guys consisted of their bikes and the clothes on their backs.

Moving out of my parents' home wasn't the traumatic experience you might imagine. In fact, it was great to be living on my own. My first problem was learning how to cook. I solved this problem the way many single guys do -- I avoided doing it, instead going to restaurants for breakfast, lunch, and dinner. When I ate at the apartment, it was sandwiches on paper plates. Fast, satisfying, and virtually no clean up.

A gourmand I was not. Everything I ate was fine, and if it wasn't, the beer would wash it down. I was working on the docks, thanks to the Teamster hiring hall

As I was adjusting to life on my own, one night I was driving down Mission with a pal, Don Clark (no relation). It was late, probably 2:30 a.m.

"Hold on, John," he said and swerved into the car alongside of us and pushed the guy over to the curb.

Don jumped out and told the guy that if he paid him 50 dollars, he wouldn't call the police. He had this driver convinced that he had hit us. The bars in California close at 2:00 a.m., and the guy was obviously drunk. Happy to avoid a potential confrontation with the police, a huge increase on his auto insurance and other problems, he gladly gave Don all the cash he had on him and drove away. This was Don's regular scam and it was how he got his drinking money.

Don was a Destruction Derby driver, and he coaxed me into trying it once. I lasted all of 10 minutes at the derby. Even when my car was disabled, I had a hard time getting out of it because cars were still crashing into me. One derby was enough for me. It was also quite a while before I drove around with Don again late at night.

Fort Funston.

Frenchy, Blackjack, and Phil came over one night to see if I wanted to go to the forts with them. Forts? Yeah, a lot of San Francisco was military installations. They were talking about Fort Funston, which occupied much of the western side of the Presidio of San Francisco (the Presidio was a military base that is now inactive, but it was operational at the time) I remembered the military had put up a fence, so no one could get into the post. They said they could fix that, and off we went.

The hills on the west side of the post faced the Pacific. There were gun emplacements to protect the city from attacks in WWII. There were also a lot of bunkers – storage rooms dug into the hills and connected by cement-lined tunnels. These were our actual destination.

When we got to the fence, Frenchy produced a pair of cutters and made quick business of the lock on the fence. It had been a long time since I had been to the forts, but they hadn't changed much. When we got into the tunnels, Phil accelerated down the dark tunnels like a bat out of hell. Blackjack took off after him, followed by Frenchy. I watched as they headed into the darkness. All of a sudden Frenchy's taillights disappeared. Where'd he go? Maybe his taillight just went out. I headed down the tunnel slowly, and then stopped. Directly in front of me was a huge hole. I found out later, the hole was there to store ammunition during the war. Someone had put a piece of plywood over it and the weight of Phil and Blackjack weakened it. There was Frenchy down at the bottom of the hole, lying on a sand pile.

Frenchy was in deep shit, perhaps seriously hurt. I yelled for Phil and Blackjack, but they couldn't hear me, because of all the noise their engines made in the tunnels. I yelled down into the hole.

"French! You all right, man?" Despite the cacophony of thundering motorcycle engines, I heard a faint moan. I jumped down into the hole and asked Frenchy where he hurt. God, what a lucky guy. He only had a few scratches. When Phil and Blackjack got back, we helped Frenchy out, and then Phil lifted Frenchy's bike out. Yeah, I said lifted. Phil was one strong guy. The night was over. We headed out to go get Frenchy's bike fixed. The way it looked and drove reminded me of the time I hit the screaming woman's house. We left the forts alone for a while after that.

The Bermuda Palms.

One of the places we liked to visit was the Bermuda Palms in San Rafael, a town 30 miles north of the Golden Gate Bridge. The owner, Whitey, was a character and he liked it when we showed up, mainly because he was always fighting with the City of San Rafael, and he knew the city did not like us around.

The Grateful Dead later had their recording studio behind the Palms, and Janis Joplin liked to hang out there. So did Mama Cass, of the Mamas and Papas. Later, she did not want to be called Mama after she split from the group, she wanted to be called Cass. Everyone knew Janis liked to drink, and she almost always had a flask of Southern Comfort in her back pocket. One night Janis got smart with a Hell's Angel, and he knocked her out cold. The Hell's Angel warned her, but she would not let up. Janis was playing the role that she thought her fans wanted, the tough-talking mama. She was really not like her stage persona.

Mama Cass liked to ride with Filthy Phil. What a sight! We were all surprised any bike could hold them both. One night, Phil was taking Mama to the Palms. He was feeling no pain, and when they got to the Palms, Mama fell to one side and both of them fell to the ground. No one laughed. You never laughed at Phil.

The Palms was a great place because it never pretended to be more than it was -- a seedy nightclub. We had a ball there, but then we had to cross the Golden Gate Bridge to get there, which meant we'd be hassled by the highway patrol, who would alert the San Rafael P.D. to take over when we entered the city limits. They were always busting us for something. There once was a San Rafael chapter of the Hell's Angels, but not since they later became the Santa Rosa chapter.

CHAPTER ELEVEN

By now, you're probably wondering why an outlaw biker guy's life would yield footprints from rock stars of the sixties. Fate. Kismet. Blind, stupid luck. All of the above. It's only guessing now, but the San Francisco Bay area in the 60s, as we used to say, is where it was happenin'. Unlike the snobbery of Los Angeles, where the rich hang out with only other rich people and/or their dope dealers, and unlike New York where the only thing different social classes have in common is their dope dealer, San Francisco was really an egalitarian scene. Rich, poor, famous, infamous, dealing, buying, sharing, grooving, getting high, feeling low – all of it was shared through the entire strata of human beings.

In some people's minds, of course, there wasn't much of a difference between bikers and rock singers. According to them, we all belonged in hell, and that's how we liked it. The social freedom movement for young people tore down barriers, opened (and closed) doors between every element of society. San Francisco, with its great liberal tradition, and its attitude of amused observation, was the perfect hatching place for whatever was new and wild in those days. So it wasn't difficult for rockers to meet bikers and become friends.

Two of the first people I met on the music scene were Janis Joplin and Vicky Cunningham. . Vicky wanted to work for Bill Graham the first time she met him. Bill had moved his business to Fillmore West on Van Ness and Market after moving from the original Fillmore on Fillmore and later would move again to Winterland. She walked in and saw this guy wiping down the bar and rushing around like a mad man. Nobody works that hard, she thought to herself. When she discovered that guy was Bill Graham and he was running his own business, she decided she wanted to work for him. She walked over to Bill and asked him for a job.

"No, not right now, but give me your number," was the response she got. Bill called her a few days later.

"You still want a job?"

"Oh, hell, yes," she said. "By the way, what is the job?"

"Counting money," he said, and hung up.

He wasn't kidding. Vicky would count the cash stacked on bread trays – a lot of bread trays. It spilled off onto the floor. Bill was making a lot of dough. (Bread trays? Dough? I'm not kidding.) He ran a cash business. Vicky would count it, stuff it in a sack, and Bill would run the sack across the street to the bank. Maybe times have changed, but back then, a lot of people saw Bill running across the street with a bag of money, dumping it in the night deposit box. They must have thought, it's Bill, the bagman. The Fillmore was a huge success. That is the most modest statement I can make about that.

Pretty soon, Bill started asking Vicky to go out with him. She said no, and she kept saying no. The way he finally got a date with her reveals a lot about Bill Graham and how he became successful in a highly competitive business.

It began when Janis Joplin died. Janis got caught in the same web that had once snared Jerry – the big H. Anyway, Bill knew how much Vicky liked Janis and asked her if she wanted to go to the wake with him. She accepted. What Bill had neglected to tell her was the wake was held the week before. She recovered from that, and they spent several years in a stormy relationship.

After Janis died, Vicky and Bill were watching a rerun of "The Tonight Show." Janis was a guest. During her interview, Bill turned to Vicky and began bragging about how many times he had slept with Janis. When he had finished his tale, Vicky looked at him a minute before she spoke.

"Why the hell would Janis want to sleep with you?"

Vicky and Janis Joplin were good friends. One day when Vicky was working at the Monterey Jazz festival, she was backstage with Janis, who was a nervous wreck, fearing the audience would not like her. After her set, she returned back-stage, beaming ear to ear. They had loved her.

When Janis left her band, Big Brother and the Holding Company, and played her first gig at Bill Graham's expanded Fillmore at Winterland with her new band, her fans turned against her. There wasn't much applause, and they didn't request an encore. Bad deal. To make matters worse, when she went out to her car, she discovered that someone had stolen it. Bill Graham immediately put out the word that whoever returned her car would receive a lifetime pass to the Fillmore. The car was returned, and Bill made good on his promise.

My First Concert.

As an activist, I asked musicians and other friends to help support worthy causes, such as fighting the California mandatory helmet law. The first concert I put on was in San Rafael. Vicky came and asked me if it was all right if she went back-stage.

"Sure, Vicky."

A little while later, backstage security called on the two-way radio to advise there was someone backstage eating all the food and drinking all the beer, which was there for the musicians. When I got backstage, there was Vicky and her girl-friend chowing down big time. I told security it was OK.

Something like that happened to Joe Buchwald, Marty Balin's father. Joe and I and some other people had gone to Marin a la Carte, where Craig Chaquico was playing. I took Joe backstage, and we introduced ourselves to the producer, who gave us backstage passes. I had to go out front, and left Joe at the food table. When I came back, Joe was being led away by two security people.

"Hey, what's up?"

"He won't stop eating the food," said security. Just then Craig came out, and told them that Joe could eat his food.

"Forget it," Joe said, and we went out front and watched the show.

Biker-Cops.

One of the guys who rode with us for quite a while later became a cop. After he got his badge, he started to bust a lot of guys in MC clubs. This didn't sit well with any of the bikers, so they came up with a plan. It called for one guy to roar by this new cop at breakneck speed. Naturally the new cop would chase him. Conveniently, there was an oil slick on the curve of the overpass approach to the freeway. The new cop took the bait and races after the speeder in hot pursuit. When he hit the oil slick, he slid from here to Monday. He didn't bother us after that incident.

Years later, something similar happened. A guy who rode with us was always breaking the law. Man, everything from hit-and-run, covering his license plate, assault, not paying tolls on the Golden Gate Bridge, and just lots and lots of bad-ass crap. One day he suddenly got religion or something, because he decided to join the California Highway Patrol. He was able to get in quite easily because he was Mexican and there was a need to meet the minority quota.

A few months later, after he'd been assigned motorcycle duty, he began busting bikers and bragging about it. The 1% club in his area found out where he hung out after work, and they proceeded to rip every piece of wiring out of his bike. The dummy didn't get the message and continued to harass bikers, and the next time, hey weren't so gentle. He found his bike burned to the ground. After that he let up somewhat.

Death Head.

In the mid-60s, Hunter S. Thompson wrote a book, based on time he spent with the Oakland Hell's Angels. He wrote about how the Oakland and Frisco Angels were at odds with each other. , Believe it or not, the conflict was over the size of the Death Head that appeared on the Hell's Angel patch. Bob Roberts wanted to keep the small Death Head; Sonny, who was president of the Oakland Angels, wanted the large Death Head. That was the entire damn reason for the years of bad blood between the two chapters.

Presidents Become Angels.

Once the Oakland Angels invited the Presidents to come and party with them at their ranch. When our club got there, they had 40 Hell's Angels waiting for the 20 members of our club. The head of the Oakland Angels told our club to turn in our patches and become Angels, or there would be trouble. Papa Ralph didn't like that ultimatum.

"Okay, let's get it on right now," but he paused. "Or we can party." They chose to party.

Pete Page, who I had sponsored into the Presidents MC, accepted their offer, and that's how the Daly City Hell's Angels started. Ralph didn't join right then, but he did later. It was Pete Page who came up with the idea to remove the individual cities from the patch and just use California on the bottom rocker. Pete's reasoning was that if they just put the state on the patch, the cops wouldn't know what area they were from to track them down.

Hunter S. Thompson.

Hunter S. Thompson accompanied the Frisco Angels up to Squaw Rock, about 100 miles north of San Francisc on a mountaintop above the Russian River. That's where they beat him up, and the word was they beat him up because he was using the Hell's Angels to create his own notoriety and cash. In fact, everyone felt he was doing just that, including George (Junkie George) Zahn.

Junkie strode up to Hunter and called him a punk. Hunter just stood there with a grin on his face. Apparently, in Hunter's crowd, that smile gave him some kind of invincibility, but not here. George beat Hunter up, and would have done more damage had Bob Roberts not stepped in. Bob Roberts was one of the smartest and best presidents the Hell's Angels had, in case you want to know.

Rip Off.

One time in Haight-Ashbury, when a hippie went up to a Hell's Nomad (an Angel who could go to any chapter, but had no home club) and handed him $ 6,000.

"Score me some acid, man," was all he said. The Nomad put the money in his pocket and left town. The hippie went to Bob Roberts with his complaint. Bob made the Nomad return to San Francisco, where he conducted a hearing at the Daly City clubhouse. The Nomad was reprimanded and the hard and fast rule came down: no

Hell's Angel would rip off anyone like that again Bob Roberts made the rule, and everyone enforced it.

Bill Graham.

I'm not through with Bill Graham, yet. Bill and the MC had set a deal: Hell's Angels didn't have to pay to get into any of his events. Somewhere along the line, Bill apparently reneged on the arrangement, and two Angels went to his office to see about that. Their method of negotiation was unique – they hung him out the office window by his ankles. When the people below saw the flashy rock and roll impresario swinging away, they began to shout. Were they calling for the police to help? Not exactly.

"Drop him! Drop him!" is what they said.

It wasn't universally known, but there were a lot of people who didn't like Bill. He once produced a Rolling Stones concert, where he set up his own entrance. All the money from ticket sales made from that entrance went into his pocket, with no share going to the Stones.

You can say what you want about Bill Graham (and a lot of people have), but if it hadn't been for him, the Grateful Dead might never have been so successful. It was Graham, along with the Hell's Angels, who produced some of the first Grateful Dead concerts. These historical concerts were held at the Longshoremen's Hall in San Francisco. They began when Bob Roberts contacted Jerry when Gino Heineke was killed by the Gypsy Jokers in the Golden Gate Park. He asked Jerry if he'd play a tribute for Gino. Jerry said yes immediately, and that was the beginning of the Grateful Dead and the Hell's Angels' long relationship.

Jerry also helped to produce the movie "Hell's Angels Forever," with Sandy Alexander, President of the New York chapter.

CHAPTER TWELVE

Listen, the Hell's Angels has had more rumors, lies, fairytales, and B. S. spread about them for so many years, that no one seems to remember what they were really like. Everything I've told you so far is true. It's too bad we didn't think to have a club historian, because much of the way people feel about the club is due to media hype and reporters' desire or need to write some lively copy, instead of the truth. There's a great deal of difference between the facts and the truth, but maybe that's another book. Right now, I'll disclose more of what I know about confrontations, run-ins with the cops, revenge (sweet and otherwise) and, as you all want to know, the truth about that murder in Altamont.

Forgotten Angels.

Even though Pete Page and Papa Ralph were responsible for starting the Daly City Hell's Angels MC, there is not one picture of them on the Daly City web site today. Most of the ex-Hell's Angels don't like to hang around the club, because a new prospect might like to take out a retired member, just to make a name for himself. If you were out of the club and your tattoo was removed, you couldn't be around the club, period. I knew one ex-Hell's Angel who was thrown out of the club. He was a good six foot, five inches, and 260 pounds. The Hell's Angels cut his tattoo off of his chest. Nobody was immune, no matter what his or her size. Some ex-Hell's Angels were told to leave the area and never come back. If you were a prospect, and you weren't accepted in the club, they kept your bike.

Juanita's Gallery.

A bunch of the Presidents were relaxing in Sausalito at Juanita's Gallery. Ralph, Pete, Darrel, and Joe Bologna were having coffee, when 10 black guys came in. The black guys sat down a couple of tables away, and all of a sudden, one of the black guys threw his drink at Ralph. The fight was on. Pete and Ralph kicked their asses before the cops came and broke it up. They made the black guys leave. Ralph, Pete, Darrel, and Joe finished their drinks and were heading for their bikes, when the same group of black guys jumped them. This time, one of them had an ax and hit Pete in the head. To this day, Pete still wears a bandana around his head to hide the scar.

Jimmy Souza.

Jimmy Souza died in 1992, and there was a huge Hell's Angel funeral. I attended with Jimmy's father, Joe. I hadn't seen Joe in a very long time and couldn't believe how old he looked, even though he still had that spark. Jimmy was one tough, but great guy, who had been brought into the club by Bob Roberts

Precita Park.

There was the time in Precita Park when 30 black guys jumped a Hell's Angel prospect. When the prospect called Bob Roberts, Bob rounded up the club and went to Precita Park. By the time the cops got there, the blacks that hadn't run away were in really bad shape. There were Bob Roberts, Jimmy Sousa, the prospect and seven other Angels against 30 black guys. When the cops checked them into the police station, there wasn't a scratch on any of the Angels.

Bob Hall was the treasurer of the Frisco Angels for about eight years, and right after he got out of the club, he came home and found a guy robbing his house. Bob beat the shit out of the man and threw him into the trunk of his car. Then he drove to a cliff and threw the guy over the edge. The man survived and came back to Bob's house, this time with a gun. When Bob came out of his house, the man fired at him, but missed. Bob ducked behind a wall, and the guy fired again. This time, the bullet hit the wall and got Bob in the eye. Now Bob has a glass eye. I don't think that guy ever shot anyone again though, because the cops hauled him away, and Bob never saw him again.

But even the toughest men suffer. About a year later, Bob was riding down a country road with his wife on the back of his bike, and a car ran them off the road. Bob's wife died in his arms. The handlebars had punctured her lungs. Some coward had it in for bikers.

Party House, Haight Ashbury.

While Bob Hall was in the club, the Hell's Angels had a party house in Haight Ashbury. Late one night a carload of black guys pulled up next door on the sidewalk and started to honk their horn. Pete Nell, who was vice president of Frisco at the time, went up to the car with Bob Hall.

"What the fuck do you think you're doing?" Pete yelled.

"Fuck you!" was the reply.

That was the wrong thing to say, and with that, Pete threw his can of beer at the driver. Pete reached through the window and punched the guy, and then about three dozen Angels poured out of the house, surrounding the car. They started to smash it, and there were Angels on the hood and on the roof. The guys in the car looked terrified. When all was done, the car was nearly flat. The people who'd been in the car were hightailing it as fast as their feet would carry them. This was not too fast, as they each had at least something broken. Bob decided they'd better get rid of the car, so they pushed it down the hill around the corner, and watched as it crashed into a car at the bottom of the hill. This little activity was followed imme-diately by the sound of police sirens in the distance. Pete and Bob started walking back to the house, when a police car pulled up along side of them. Two cops jumped out and grabbed Bob and handcuffed him. Then they tried to do the same to

Pete.

"Fuck this! I'm not going to jail," Pete said.

Pete hit one cop and knocked him out, as Angels poured out of the house and started to fight the cops. Four more police cars arrived, and in the confusion Bob made a break for the house, still handcuffed. Inside, one of the Angels suggested that they go over the back fence. It would have been impossible for Bob to climb the fence, so Ron Secully said he'd catch Bob if the others would help him over the fence. Ron climbed over and waited to catch Bob, but the cops grabbed him. When Bob came over the fence, it was the cops who caught him. Surprise, surprise.

The cop, who had cuffed Bob, took him back into the house, and with the help of three other cops, dragged him into the kitchen, where they began to beat him with their clubs.

"Think you're a tough guy, don't you?" they taunted.

"You can't hurt me! I'm a Hell's Angel!" Bob flung back at them. The cops began to hit Bob harder, not realizing Bob didn't feel much, because he was pretty drunk.

Most of the Hell's Angels were rounded up and put into paddy wagons, but it took almost 100 of San Francisco's finest to do it.

Hell's Angel's Merchandise.

The Hell's Angels fiercely protected their name and logo. They didn't allow anyone to sell anything that resembled their identification without their approval, and their enforcement policies were strict and unforgiving. One day, one of the Angels was instructed to drive to a store about 50 miles from San Francisco and strip the merchandise off the shelves there. The Angels had received word the store was selling merchandise that looked like Hell's Angels stuff. There was one more instruction. "Break the guy's nose, to teach him a lesson."

The Angel found the shop and removed all the merchandise, but felt sorry for the guy who was crying who claimed that he didn't know anything about rules concerning the logo, so the Angel gave him the benefit of the doubt and did not break his nose.

When the Angel returned to the clubhouse, he was asked if he broke the guy's nose. When he said he hadn't, another Angel jumped on his bike and went to the store and broke the guy's nose.

It may sound harsh, but it was the only way the Hell's Angels could protect their name. Corporations sue if someone uses their name or logo, which is what the Hell's Angels would probably do today. Back then, though, Angels didn't deal with lawyers, only bail bondsmen.

The Altamont Murder – 1969.

Probably more has been written about the Hell's Angels murder of a Rolling Stones concert-goer in 1969, than any other single event in the history of the organization. I want to tell you what happened, but not as a journalist – God knows not many of them got it right, nor understood the reasons it happened, nor bothered to examine what might have happened, if the Angels had not acted as they did. What could have happened is that Mick Jagger could have gotten killed.

Between 40 to 50 Hell's Angels left for Altamont Pass, which was 60 miles north of San Francisco on the way towards Stockton to provide security for the Stones' concert. Most rode their bikes, but some, rode in the Hell's Angels bus. When they reached the concert site, they staked out their area and started to party. At one point, one of the Hell's Angels was urinating along the side of the Hell's Angels' bus, when he glanced over to see some guy from the audience urinating on the bus.

"What the fuck do you think you're doing?" he asked.

"What does it look like?" That was the wrong thing to say. Bob zipped himself, and turned to the guy.

"What are you doing pissing on my bus?" This time he didn't wait for an answer. He told the guy to leave and then escorted him outside the Hell's Angels compound, after slapping him a few times and kicking him in the ass. When the guy was walking away, the guys inside the compound yelled for him not to fuck with Hell's Angels. No one else entered the Angel's compound that day; not after they saw what happened.

As the concert progressed, everyone was in a great mood. Then Santana came on, and their music seemed to signal a change in the mood of the crowd – and not one for the better. Fights began to break out in the audience, and there was a general nasty mood over the entire hillside. By the time the Rolling Stones came on, the audience seemed primed for something besides music.

The Hell's Angels gathered at the stage to keep people from mobbing the band, which is what they were hired to do. Despite their presence, the inadequate and poor planning of the concert's organizers hampered their job. The stage was too low and, too accessible, and it had no barriers. The Hell's Angels became the fall guys in a tragic incident that was caused as much by the poorly organized stage setup and inadequate security concerns as by anything else.

Here's what went down.

One of the Hell's Angels saw someone heading for the stage with a gun. A shot was fired. The Angel leaped over some people and stabbed the man. The stabbing shocked the world, but you have to ask yourself what would have happened if he had reached the stage and shot Mick Jagger? He put himself between what appeared to be a target and a man with a gun. What was he supposed to do then?

Have a nice chat with the gun-toting man at the rock concert? Let him shoot Mick Jagger, because he didn't like his lips? A man with a gun can usually be construed to be a man with a mission. The police, the FBI, the Secret Service, no one assumes such a person is on a mission of peace.

None of this made any difference. Had the man not been stopped, and had he killed Mick Jagger, the Hell's Angels would have been blamed for not doing their job. What most reports didn't include is the fact that Bob Roberts was standing next to Mick on stage, and his life was in peril, too. Was it protection or was it swift, justifiable action? Violent death is always a tragedy, and the events of Altamont may be debated for decades. What happened, of course, was the media chose this sad event to blame the Hell's Angels for bringing to an end the entire peace and love movement. That's a crock. The movement had run its course by then. Social revolutions don't last long in America. Something new comes along to catch the public's attention, grab the headlines, fill the television screen. A new generation, or half-generation, comes along to replace "the old."

I have always believed the reason why the Grateful Dead lasted so long was because Jerry and the band carried the 60s with them into the future. I spoke with Jerry about this into the 70s. He said he simply did not understand why the Dead was so popular for so long. I told him it was because they'd brought the message of peace and love with them. Unless you were at a Dead concert to experience it, you missed that feeling. It wasn't the drugs, but the sincerity of the people there, who really did want peace and love in the world. Many of the kids I met at Dead concerts in later years were like butterflies, fragile and beautiful. And, as is the case so many times, there were bad apples, and it was the druggy, strung-out ones who killed the grand experiment, and there were fewer of those than you'd believe.

Fillmore Auditorium.

I walked into the Fillmore the day Bill Graham opened it. The first thing I saw was a very nervous Bill Graham. At the front was a barrel of apples. I grabbed one on my way up the stairs. In the auditorium, I discovered why Bill was nervous. As soon as you walked in, you got stoned from the heavy clouds of industrial-grade pot smoke. It reminded me of "Apocalypse Now," – a world of weed-induced pacifism that believed, "Man, let's stay stoned and maybe everything will get better."

I'm telling you this now because almost 30 years later (1994), when they reopened the Fillmore, it was almost as if nothing had changed. Old people sat on the floor, just as they had 30 years earlier. There were many empty spaces on the floor, signifying people who were either dead or no longer in the area. It was not a happy scene. It was more of a sad confirmation that those times had not changed anything. The pot smoke, the apples, the light shows, the magic of it was gone, all gone. I sat on the floor with Joe Buchwald and said, "Joe, it failed." He just nodded.

"Peace and love did not take over the world, Joe."

He nodded again. "It wasn't even a transition, man."

Moose Dies.

I was working in Los Angeles and visiting my parents in San Francisco, when I received word Moose was dead. I jumped in my car and headed for Moose's house, hoping to hell it wasn't true. It was. I asked his younger brother how it happened.

"They found him hanging in a closet." He paused and gathered himself together once again. "They ruled it a suicide." I could not believe Moose would hang himself, but his brother believed it, so I let it go. My memories of Moose were filled with laughter and fun, of times we got giggle-assed stoned, and even of all the fights we got into because of his reputation.

There was one night in particular. Moose and I were walking down Mission Street, on our way to the Squeeze Inn, one of our hangouts. We were just walking and four guys were coming towards us. We swerved towards the curb to let them pass, but they kept moving towards us. When we were close, one of them shouted, "Hey, Moose, you can't be as bad as they say." Uh-oh, I thought to myself as Moose knocked out the first guy who approached. I hit the second guy, but did not knock him down. I went back after him, as Moose worked on the other two.

We were doing OK, but all of a sudden this guy came running from across the street and knocked one of the guys out, and then took a swing at Moose and then at me, after which he took off running towards Ocean Avenue. By now, some of our friends were on the scene, and we chased the sock-and-run guy. I was the fastest, and I caught up with him at a t hamburger stand. Just as I got to him, he turned around. That surprised me, and I slipped and fell to the sidewalk. Before he could do any damage, the other guys arrived. Now Moose told all of us to hold the guy down, which we did. Moose hit him with everything he had. Oooh.

The guy just shook his head and smiled. Double oooh. If Moose couldn't knock him out, we would all be in trouble. There could have been a very sad ending to this story, but you have to remember it was our turf and here came John Bacaluppi, who pulled his car to the curb, so that Moose and I could jump in the car and head out. In front of City College, a car pulled alongside us and rolled down a window. It's the guy Moose hit.

"Hey, Moose, I want you. One-on-one." Moose tells John to stop the car. Moose climbs out, and the next thing we knew, Moose was on the ground. Not possible. Moose had never been taken down. Never. Moose gets up and then gets knocked down again. This guy was s good. Four more times of getting knocked down and with his nose broken, I step in.

"Give it up, Moose." He didn't want to, but eventually John and I talk him into it.

I didn't see the other guy again -- until about 10 years later. I ran into him in a restaurant in North Beach. I talked to him for a while, then reminded him about our sidewalk encounter 10 years earlier.

"Yeah, Moose was one tough customer."

"You were pretty tough yourself. Nobody before or after you ever knocked him down."

"Thank you," he said. And that was the last I ever saw of him.

After Moose's funeral a few of us went down to the Squeeze Inn. I spotted a guy there who looked familiar, but I couldn't place him. He said his name was Pablo. He said he lived in the same neighborhood as Moose, on Courtland, which was mostly Mexican. I still could not place him. I returned to my friends, and then overheard this Pablo character say to someone that Moose was dead before he was on the rope.

"What did you say?"

"About what, man?"

"About Moose being dead before he was on the rope. What did you mean?"

"I did not say that." he said,

"I heard you. Tell me what the fuck you meant."

"Leave it alone," he said. "You might find yourself some trouble."

In that instant, I remembered where I knew him from. He was one of the guys who had hung out at the Cherokee Bar on Courtland. It was almost as if he could see I had remembered, and he took off out the back door and was over the fence and gone.

The next day, I called a friend at the SFPD and asked him to check the coroner's report on Moose. Naturally, he wanted to know why. I told him it might have been a murder. He got back to me and said he could find nothing to indicate it was murder, and that it would remain on the books as a suicide. Years later, I learned Moose had been heavily involved with drug dealers, that he screwed someone, and they had killed him. We never found out who it was.

Hollywood Bowl.

By 1968, I'd moved to Los Angeles and lost touch with Jerry, but remained in contact with Cliff. By now I was married with two kids and studying acting. Living in LA was pretty wild. We lived two blocks from Whiskey-A-Go-Go on the Sunset strip. Everyone we met seemed to be on acid, or wishing they were. We met a lot of musicians and would go to their homes to watch them rehearse. One day it was the Doors, the next day, the Byrds, or almost any headliner you could name from the 60s.

Mama Cass Elliot lived nearby on Mt. Olympus, so I saw her a lot. I reminded her of the night she took the spill with Filthy Phil, but she obviously wanted to forget those days.

I was constantly surprised by the amount of acid people were using in those days. It was the era of Timothy Leary's "Turn on, tune in, drop out" lifestyle. By this time, Leary was incarcerated, but I had become friends with his attorney, who visited Leary in jail. Apparently, the High Priest of High told his mouthpiece he had to get him out of there. If he did not get him out of there, he said, he would be forced to go over the wall. Oh yeah, when he went over the wall, he added, he was going to leave his body behind.

A lot of the San Francisco experience trickled down to Tinseltown. The aura generated by Bill Graham, Jefferson Airplane, and the Grateful Dead was pure enough when it started, but by the time it had sifted down to LA, it had become diluted.

The Dead scheduled a concert at the Hollywood Bowl. I had heard a lot of rumors that Jerry had taken a lot of acid trips and was not in good shape at all. I wanted to check that out and see how much he'd changed. Most of my reports had come from Cliff, but the media had begun reporting stuff, too.

I waited backstage, a little nervous, not knowing what to expect. Jerry pulled up in a pickup truck. When he stepped out, I wasn't sure if he wanted to speak to me. His hair was wild, and he had a faraway look. I wasn't even sure he recognized me.

"Hey, Jer," I said as he walked past me.

"John! How are you?" I held my hand out. We shook hands, but his hand was dead-fish limp. I feared Jerry'd blown his mind, but he seemed to remember me.

"John, you staying for the show? Let me get you a backstage pass."

"Sure, Jer. Thanks." I wanted to see and hear for myself what the Dead had become, and also check out Jerry's performance. . I stood in the wings and watched and listened and all my doubts disappeared. Jerry played brilliant guitar. He was fantastic and the audience realized it. The ease and clarity of his playing reassured me Jerry Garcia was at the top of his game.

I didn't hang around for the whole concert. I'd seen enough to restore my faith in my buddy. At the time, I didn't realize it would be some time before I saw either Cliff or Jerry again.

CHAPTER THIRTEEN

I began traveling around North America and Hawaii, selling advertising. I was out of touch with Cliff and Jerry, but on a trip to Cleveland, I saw in the paper the Dead would be performing there. I decided to go see Jerry do his thing.

I stopped at a restaurant across the street from the auditorium to get a bite before the show. The guy sitting at the counter next to me asked if I had any tickets to the show.

"I don't need tickets. I'm going backstage."

"Do you know Jerry?" he asked, about to pee in his pants.

"Yes." I wasn't able to figure the kid out because at the time I didn't have a clue as to what a Deadhead was. I was soon to find out.

"C-could I go with you?" he asked, Christmas in his eyes.

"What the hell, why not? What's your name?"

"Jimmy," he said.

I got backstage and was looking around for Jerry when a security guy asked me what I was doing there.

"I'm a friend of Jerry's," I said.

"Yeah, sure you are. You're going to have to leave." Just then Jerry walked in and saw Jimmy and me.

"Give them backstage passes," he said. Jimmy was about to faint. His reaction to Jerry reminded me of the first time I sat in the audience to see the Dead. It was a New Year's Eve show at the Oakland Coliseum. My date was more used to going to the ballet and opera. She kept yelling, "(Sit) down in front!" I had to explain.

"This is what they do at a Dead show. They get up and dance. " As I was explaining, the music stopped and someone next to me turned to my date and said quiet please.

"Jerry is going to speak." He said it in the hushed tones generally reserved for the gods.

"John, I gotta get ready, but we can talk at break." Jimmy and I stood in the wings, as I had done at the Hollywood Bowl, and once again I was simply blown away. Jerry had gotten even better. Jimmy was too excited to say a damn word.

When the set was over, Jerry stopped and said, "Let's go to the dressing room." I followed Jerry and Phil to the dressing room, and left Jimmy backstage, or as he had begun to call it, Seventh Heaven. We talked. He was still the Jerry I knew as a kid, but man, he looked tired. Beat.

"Jerry, do you know where Cliff is?" I asked.

"No, I don't." Phil Lesh said he thought he was living in Marin.

"Jerry, he's still your brother. Listen, the only people who really care about you are your family."

"What about you and your brother?" he said. My brother was my half-brother.

"We never got along, but that's different."

"What's different about it?" Jerry demanded. I had no answer. "Besides," he continued, "Cliff and I have nothing common. If we got together we'd bore each other to death."

Jerry was getting upset. Maybe he was thinking about the time Cliff chopped off his finger. That happened before Jerry's father died. Jerry was only four when it happened. He and Cliff were chopping wood, and there was an accident. That was pretty traumatic stuff for a preschooler. Or maybe he was remembering how the big kids on Harrington Street had treated us. Who knows? You can't live in another man's head, even if you grew up on the same block together. He still had another set and some encores to do.

"Jerry... good seeing you again." He nodded, and we hugged each other. I watched him return to the stage. It would be quite a while before I would see him again.

In the meantime on a trip to visit my parents, I contacted Cliff. He was living in Fairfax in Marin County, north of San Francisco, and working for the post office, married, with two daughters at the time.

We set a time to meet for lunch. Cliff looked pretty much the same. Right off, I started to tell him about my conversation with Jerry in Cleveland. Cliff became upset before I had 10 words out of my mouth.

"Please, John, I don't want to hear it."

"Why, Cliff? He's still your brother. I made peace with my brother. After I talked to Jerry in Cleveland, I called my brother and went to his house . . . "

"John, just leave it alone, please."

"OK, Cliff," I said. Somehow we made it through the lunch, but it was obvious I wasn't the guy to get Jerry and Cliff Garcia back together. The realization of that was one of the saddest moments of my life. When we finished, I asked Cliff if the two of us could stay in touch.

"Sure, John."

I did see Jerry again. At the Stone in Berkeley, and it was the Jerry Garcia Band playing this time, not the Grateful Dead. I went into the dressing room, and there was Jerry. Whatever difficult feelings he'd had in Cleveland were behind him now, and he seemed to be in genuinely good spirits.

"Hey, John, how are you?"

"Good, Jerry. And you?" I had to ask because Jerry still did not look good. I told Jerry that, and he became visibly upset, so I switched to small talk and he calmed down. We chatted until it was time for him to go on.

It was startling to see Jerry Garcia performing with only about 40 people in the audience. There was something else, too, something I hadn't spotted before. This marked the first time I ever saw a trace of arrogance in Jerry. He walked to the stage as if he were royalty. I heard him say to someone, "I've seen more people in a toilet."

However, his musical instincts were intact. I later saw him at the Stone on Broadway in San Francisco. This time the crowd was much larger. The JGB had developed a strong and growing fan base. I went backstage and said hello, but we didn't talk. Jerry was creating something beyond the Grateful Dead, and he was chasing his new dream for all his was worth.

Cliff goes to work for the Dead.

There was progress, though. Cliff was hired by the Dead organization to work in their merchandise department. It was a start, both for Cliff to become associated with Jerry's business, and for their rift, whatever it was, to begin repairing itself. The first merchandise department was a tiny building in San Rafael. Now it's a huge warehouse up Highway 101 in Novato. (Cliff still works there and Jerry ultimately remembered him in his will. Maybe I did get through to Jerry, after all.)

Broadway Tunnel Races – 1990.

The Broadway Tunnel in San Francisco is a - twin tube, four-lane, tiled tunnel that used to mark the border between the Italian section of the city, North Beach, and Chinatown. Tourists, drunks and teenagers honked their car horns when going though it, but we used it for something different.

I used to race Bob Roberts through the Broadway Tunnel, and no matter what he was riding, I could never beat him. I warned him one day that I would buy the world's fastest Harley just to beat his ass. He laughed. He could ride like no one I had ever raced. If there was ever such a thing as a man and a machine becoming one entity, it was Bob Roberts on a Harley. No one had ever beaten him that I knew of.

We were screwing around North Beach one night at the Coffee Gallery on Grant Avenue. I was the proud owner of a new bike, a Sportster 1200. It was fast, period. Fast. A Hell's Angel was at the Coffee Gallery bragging how fast his bike was.

"You want to find out how fast your bike really is?" I asked him.

"Broadway Tunnel," he said.

We went to one end of the tunnel and halted traffic. It wasn't difficult; no one told a Hell's Angel what to do. The Angel started to smoke his back tire. I just waited. You could do the show or you could do the go. We got the signal and screamed off the start-line. My front tire was off the ground. I was doing a wheelie, and by the time my front tire came back down, the Angel was halfway through the tunnel. All I saw was a ball of flame bellowing from his exhaust. When I caught up with him, he was stopped at the other end of the tunnel.

"How about another shot?" I asked.

"Fuck, yes."

We turned our bikes around to go the other way in the tunnel. I was going to make sure I kept my front tire on the ground this time. Another tires screaming. This time, I kept the front tire on the ground and looked in my mirror and saw the Angel way behind me. I had beaten him, pure and simple. I felt great, until he coasted up to me and told me he'd run out of gas. He pushed his bike back to the Coffee Gallery, but I didn't go back there. I found out later, the Angel I raced was Mark Perry, out of Oakland. He asked everyone if they knew who I was. "John Clark," they told him. It turned out Perry had not run out of gas, but had blown his engine.

Years later, it was reported he had fallen off his bike and was run over by a semi. I don't believe there is any possibility that was true. Mark Perry was too good of a rider. My theory is that someone he knew kicked him off his bike. And, yes, you're right, the police don't spend a lot of time on accidents that kill bikers.

Armadillo's 1990.

One of the places we liked to hang out in later years was the Armadillo on Fillmore. It had one pool table, beer, and wine, and little else, but it was a great place to hang out. Some nights, there might be 50 bikes out front. It was quite a mix from earlier years. There were all kinds of punkers coming into the bar, with their hair every color you could imagine, and every part of their bodies pierced. These apes also seemed to have inherited most of Haight Street, replacing the sweet hippie kids. No flower children now. A violent element reflected in their dress, their music and their attitude, but they didn't bother bikers, and we left them alone to their own edgy lives.

Then the fucking impossible happened. The owner decided to open a sushi bar. Bob Roberts went wild.

"We are not hanging out anywhere they serve raw fish!" We moved our socializing to a bar on Haight Street. Just to show you how all things can change, years later Bob Roberts learned to like sushi, big time.

Flight or Fight.

One night in 1991, after some heavy drinking, I pulled up along side two Hell's Angels at a stop sign. Being a mellow fellow, I gave them a wave and blasted out of the hole, and drove to one of my favorite bars for a final finale. Before I could get off my bike, the two Angels stopped across the street and motioned me over to them. I got back on my bike, thinking, (OK, unclearly) maybe they had a problem. One of them named Kelly gave me the scoop.

"No one buzzes Hell's Angels like that."

"I didn't buzz you guys," I said. With that, Kelly tried to grab my handlebars. I hit his arms away.

"What the fuck's wrong with you?" With that I took off. No final finale, but they didn't follow me, either.

A couple of nights later, I came around a turn and hit some black sand. I went one way; my bike went the other, sliding on its side down the street, sparks flying. Two friends of mine, who worked for the Angels (Frisco Choppers) came by and helped me get the bike up. They suggested we go to Morty's, one of our hang-outs in North Beach.

"They got some first aid there, and you can patch up." When I walked in, I saw two Angels that I had seen from a couple of nights back. And with them, was that Kelly guy.

I was ready for anything, despite a hell of a lot of pain from the accident and my bleeding knee. "I hope you know what you did wrong," he smirked.

"I didn't do anything wrong!"

"OK, let's shake on it." We shook hands, and I headed to the kitchen to get some first aid.

Lynn's Morty owned the place. She got me fixed up, and I returned to the bar and got a Coke. I was standing by myself, when all of a sudden Kelly walked up.

"Hey, you're not drinking. Either go outside with me or leave, and we're going to trash your bike." I didn't say anything. I went outside and moved my bike around the corner and went back inside Morty's. The second I walked in, Kelly confronted me again.

"Didn't I tell you to get the fuck out of here?" Then he slapped me. It was automatic – I hit his arm away.

"You fucking hit me!" he screamed.

"No shit, Dick Tracy." I made a quick assessment. I looked at the other two Angels for their response. My pals who brought me here could not back me up, because they worked for the Angels. My choices were simple: escalate or walk, fight or flight.

I walked.

CHAPTER FOURTEEN

Bob Roberts is remembered and honored by the Frisco Hell's Angels. Had it not been for Bob, there wouldn't have been a San Francisco chapter. The clubhouse today is nothing like the garages we met in. Now it's two stories high, with a bar and stage, and it's right behind a police station. I was at the clubhouse for the World Run in 1994One of the events Frisco set up for everyone was a ride on the Red & White Fleet. These are tour boats of San Francisco Bay. The Hell's Angels are known as the Red & White -- it's their colors. I had been there about two hours, when guess who confronts me? If you said Kelly, you get the cigar.

"What are you doing here?"

"What does it look like, Kelly? I continued on down the stairs, Kelly right behind me. Everyone knew Kelly was famous for sucker punches, so I kept my eye on him and headed for the door. I didn't want to start anything here. If Kelly popped me, everyone else would have to also, even if they were my friends. When I got to the door, Wayne, who was president of Frisco, stood there. He asked me if I was having a good time.

"Great," I said. "But I have to split." I did not say anything about Kelly. I got on my bike and drove home. I was lucky to get out of there. Kelly was one crazy guy, and there was doubt in my mind we'd meet again.

Sure enough. My next run-in with Kelly was at the clubhouse. Late one night, about 10 of us decided to go to the clubhouse. The group included Bob Roberts, Tommy Roberts, Jimmy Red, Tony, and some others. When we walked in, there was Kelly just standing there by the bar, and Papa Mark lay on the couch. From the moment we entered, Kelly was watching me like a lion watching a wounded gazelle. He was smart enough not to dare do anything with Bob Roberts there. We stayed for a while and decided to leave. As we left, Kelly yelled out to Tony that he wanted to talk to him. He went back into the clubhouse, and Kelly slammed the door.

"Wonder what that's all about," I said to Bob.

"Don't know, John."

After about 10 minutes, Tony emerged. I asked him what was going on.

"He just wants me to do him a favor," said Tony. I found out later what that favor was.

Motorcycle Service.

In 1994, Bob Roberts started a group called the Motorcycle Service. Our meeting place was at Tony's. It was a great place with slot machines, a pool table, and other games. Our patch was going to be Bob's Motorcycle Service.

I told Mark, a neighbor of mine about our group, and he sounded interested, so I had him come to a meeting. He liked what he saw, and the others liked him. He was voted into the group after coming to a few meetings. Mark worked at a local television station. When we had our first party at Morty's, he got the station to donate a great door prize – a round trip for two to Cabo San Lucas. Not bad! Tom Perkins, who owns Dudley-Perkins Harley, the oldest Harley dealership in the world, gave some great door prizes also, like leather chaps and tee- shirts; lots of good stuff. Tom, a great guy, had donated quite a few door prizes for my concert.

And, our first party turned out great. There was a tense moment or two when my girlfriend, Donna, won the trip to Cabo. I had to talk fast, because I was the one who put the event together, and it looked like the fix was in. However, Donna had bought a lot of raffle tickets, so they were convinced that there was no inside stuff going on.

After each meeting, we would go ride. It was like the old days, except now we did not have the plates on our boots, so no fireworks. On the other hand, we really moved. We flew over the hills. If you've never been on a ride, you can't imagine the experience. If you've never been on a roller coaster, you can't explain that, either.

We had 15 members now, and almost everywhere we went we got respect. We went to one club on Fillmore, right across the street from the Fillmore Auditorium. It was a place called Jack's, and the people there gave us respect. After all these years, we finally did not have to hang out at coffee shops and biker bars. We could go anywhere, because by now, a lot of people wanted to be like us. It made life a lot easier …most of the time.

There was a non-biker bar in North Beach. Our club went there together. I was inside with Bob Roberts, and the rest of the guys were still parking. I spotted a great-looking chick at the bar and struck up a conversation with her. She seemed friendly, but after a few minutes a guy (her boyfriend, I surmised) came over and said, "Move your ass." I did, thinking she was his. However, as soon as I moved, he ordered me to move again.

"You're fucking with the wrong guy," I said. He didn't seem to care. Tom Roberts had come in and was watching the whole thing. I moved a little farther away in the interest of peace, and the guy backed off some. A little while later, after some rude comments and a lot of glaring on his part, the guy walked out to the parking lot to get something from his car. When he returned, he was holding a bloody handkerchief to his face. Somebody had broken his nose. That somebody also told him he had better learn some respect for us. People don't push us around, or treat us like scum. The guy never said a word and left as soon as he could.

Jacky's Birthday.

Tony, Mark, and Pete Page went to Jacky's birthday party. Jacky was Jerry's secretary. We accumulated quite a few stares from the people at the party, because no one knew who I was. That happened a lot, even to Cliff, Jerry's brother. It was one of the reasons Cliff didn't like to hang out at the concerts. A lot of people who worked for the Grateful Dead thought they were the Dead, and they had some pretty bad attitudes. Some were just there for the ride, and did not even care for Jerry. Jacky, Oley, and Dennis McNalley were the exceptions. Anyway, most of the people at the party looked at us like we were scum, but we had fun anyway. For one thing, Pete was used to it, and he did not let it bother him. Tony was talking with someone who I did not recognize, but there were lots of people I did not recognize there. Tony didn't bother to introduce us. Later, I found out why.

The .45.

One night, Mark, the television guy, decided he wanted to go to San Francisco to see some of the hangouts from the early days. We were both living in Marin, so we took off for the city. Our first stop was the bar that used to be Mario's. I got off my bike first. There was a Hell's Angel at the door. He opened the door for me, and then he saw my patch.

"Hey, what's with the patch?" I noticed there were about 20 Hell's Angels in the back at tables. They looked like they were all Oakland, and Mark Perry was one of them. I saw a friend of mine sitting at the bar.

"What's up, Elliot?" No response.

I told the Hell's Angel at the door to talk with Bob Roberts, the president of our group. Something about the time and place didn't feel right. I knew Mark was packing a .45, and he was on record as having stated that if anyone said anything to him about his patch, he would blow them away. I headed out the door, told Mark to get back on his bike, and for us to get the hell out of there. Mark obviously did not understand the urgency of the situation.

I got on my bike and turned the corner, which was Harrington Street. I started down the hill that I knew so well for so many years. I looked in my mirror and did not see Mark, so I circled the block. When I got to Mario's, his bike was not there. Damn, they must have grabbed him. I sped off for Bob Roberts' house.

Bob was not there, but his brother Tom was.

"I think the Angels grabbed Mark." Tom was in the Motorcycle Service, and had been in the Angels many years before. He grabbed his jacket, and we were at the door, when Mark pulled up. I breathed a sigh of relief.

"I got lost," he yelled. "I went straight on Mission when you turned right."

At the next meeting, Mark told Tony about what happened. That's all Tony wanted to hear. He asked the club to take away my patch for abandoning Mark. Tony had me where he wanted me. Now he could not get rid of the one person Bob listened to, a friend he'd known for a lot of years. I stood up.

"The hell with this!" I turned in my patch. "No hard feelings, guys."
I walked out of the clubhouse and never returned.

Later, when I was moving to Washington, DC, Bob Roberts came over to give me a hand. After we were done, he said he had something for me. We went to his car, and he pulled out my patch and handed it to me, and said that my patch should never have been yanked. Thanks, Bob.

Redwood Run – 1994.

The first time I went to the Redwood Run, it was a real eye opener. The cops did not hassle us as they did in the old days because now almost everyone was riding a Harley; doctors, lawyers, judges, politicians, and even the police themselves. If cops got stopped for speeding or almost anything else, they just flashed their tin and away they would go. They were supposed to be written up with some kind of internal thing, but I knew a lot of off-duty cops so drunk they could hardly get their kickstand up. They were stopped and released as soon as they showed ID. On the way up, I was racing a friend of mine. We were clocking over a 100 miles an hour. Out of the corner of my eye, I caught a glimpse of a black and white, so I let off the throttle and a highway patrol shot by us, obviously in search of bigger fish to fry.

When we got to the Redwood Run there must have been at least 10,000 bikes. Maybe more. We then headed for the pit, my mind taking me back to the pits at China Camp 30 years earlier. But this was different. Everyone camped out and, it was a lot different from when we used to come here. We pitched our tents and headed for the beer line and the river. It was one hot day. At least that hadn't changed. The Angels had their site all set up, so I went over to say hello. Rudy and Wayne and JR were there. Rudy handed me a beer, I hung with them a while, then split for town with Bob Herbert, Roy, and two other friends.

The road seemed familiar, but when we got to town, I could not believe how much it had changed. We headed for the local bar. This time it was filled with bikers, not lumberjack types. I don't know if you can count that as a sign of progress, since most of the bikers were RUBS – Rich Urban Bikers.

It was great camping out again with all the Bros, but there was something lacking. I couldn't identify what it was at first, but then I realized that most of the people were just playing the biker game. They had money, and they went out and bought a Harley and all the accessories and clothes that went with it. They wanted to be like us, but did not want to pay the price that we had. They would be doing a scene, man. If their bike broke down, they called a service to come and fix it. Not like in the old days, when we would call one of our bros, and he would be there for us. We fixed our bikes with bailing wire, soap, gum, you name it. Now anybody with a lot of cash could become an instant biker.

It went past that. Some of the guys who are still around from the old days are riding dressers, with cell phones in one hand, going home to their computers. When I saw Papa Ralph on his dresser, I was stunned. "Never thought I'd see you on a dresser, man." Ralph looked at me for a long minute.

"Look, John, I don't laugh at your sportster, so don't laugh at my road machine." That was that. A sure sign of the times. I never thought I would see Papa Ralph on a full Dress either, but he is. I was having to make a tough adjustment.

It was a good time, the Redwood Run. There was great music and good food, and it was great to see a lot of people I had not seen in a long time. Chico was there, hiding under the trees. He did not want the Hell's Angels to see him, so he kept a low profile. No problem.

At the end of the three days, it was time to head home. I went over to Wayne, the President of Frisco, and asked him if I could ride back with them. The crowd I had ridden up with was headed for Lake Tahoe, not back to San Francisco. Also, I wanted to see if the Angels still rode fast and hard like we had done. Wayne OK'd me; we were all set to go. Half the club was going in an opposite direction. It occurred to me that if anything happened, the police would not get the whole chapter. That did not prove to be the case.

All 15 of us hit the road, and like in the old days, there was the highway patrol lurking. We were moving at least 80 mph, two by two. I brought up the rear with one other non-patch holder. Man, the ride was great. Memories of the old days just tumbled into my mind as we tooled along. Maybe it was the old-days images, but I kept waiting for the cops to make their move, to swoop down on us and start checking warrants and generally hassling us.

But nothing. For 200 glorious miles, we were doing 80 mph and not one cop in sight. The squares in cars got their thrills, too, seeing 15 Hell's Angels fly past them. Little kids in the cars pointed to us, and I could see they were laughing and waving. After all this time, did the Angels finally achieve respect from the cops? Apparently so, because in the old days we would be face-down on the side of the road, in hand cuffs. This was great!

When we got to my turnoff, I pulled up to the front and gave Wayne a wave and turned off at my exit. All of them waved back. It was a great thrill to ride like that again, a thrill reborn from the old days.

But everything wasn't that glowing. Two of the guys in the club at that time are in prison. The story was one of them was set up by the feds. Nobody ever quite got the story of what happened. Kelly is no longer in the club.

Concert Pt. Reyes, 1993.

In 1993 I put on a benefit concert to help the fight against the California mandatory helmet law. This was my second concert, the first coming six months earlier. It was Fly Like an Eagle and it was very successful.

Our group was named Personal Freedom Advocates. When I started it, there were only four of us. Now there were about 75 people who attended our weekly meetings, and it was an interesting group, a group people said would never agree on anything and never-ever get together. But I had Chico, past president of Gypsy Jokers on security, along with Pete Page, past president of Hell's Angels, Daly City; Bob Hall, Hell's Angels, Frisco; Buddha, Hell's Angels of Daly City; Papa Ralph, Hell's Angels, Daly City; Vic, Daly City, and representatives from many other bay area biker groups. Rock Sculley, Grateful Dead manager for 21 years, was also there, even if he showed up stoned most of the time.

Randy Forrester, at that time was with Elvin Bishop, now with Eddie Money, helped me big time, asking many of his musician friends to play the concert. There was also Donny Baldwin, drummer for Starship, and later for the Jerry Garcia band. Donny got Lydia Pense and Cold Blood for the concert.

We're not talking about a few little old ladies and cucumber sandwiches here. These were people who could make things happen. The meetings got so big, I had to start using a PA system. Steve Boyle was my vice president, and Paul Conroy was stage manager. We had the right people, great people, but finding a concert site for several thousand people was a bit tougher.

The first location I found was the Saloon, an historic bar in Pt. Reyes, an hour or so up the coast from San Francisco. The Saloon owner said we could block off the street, and hold it right in town. That had great appeal, so we began planning for the concert at Pt. Reyes. We had to go through the Marin County Commission for permission, but we received approval, thanks to Judy the owner of the Saloon who helped wade through a lot of red tape.

I called a friend, Warren Hinckle, who was also friendly with Hunter Thompson, and asked if he would write a story about it for his paper, the San Francisco Chronicle. I needed some ink in order to be able to sell some advertising for the concert. Hinkle wrote a story, but what a story! He made it appear that 3,000 Hell's Angels would be thundering into Pt. Reyes for a concert-party. Don't let anyone ever tell you any publicity is fine, as long as they spell your name right. The newspaper story panicked the town and they pulled our permit. It looked like we were dead meat.

Almost immediately, Judy called and said she had a ranch just a mile out of town and we could use it. It was on county property, and the town had no jurisdiction. I sent Steve Boyle out to take a look. He hated it.

"It's a quarry filled with a lake, and it's full of heavy equipment. We aren't going to be stuck in any bone yard!" I had to go look for myself. Steve wasn't wrong, but he'd rushed to judgment. There was potential here to make the location a great venue.

"First, we drain the lake," I told Steve. He looked at me like I was crazy, "No way the EPA would ever allow it."

"So we won't tell them."

And we didn't. I told Judy we'd accept her offer. It took us two months to clean the site. We dug trenches to drain the water, and EPA, if you're reading this, we didn't cause any damage. We worked on the site right up until show time. Then things really got bad. The day before the concert, there was a heavy thunderstorm, and the quarry began filling up with water again. The great, hardworking crew might have been discouraged, but they kept going. They were on top of the quarry digging trenches to divert water away from the quarry, so the building crew could finish the stage. When the first concertgoer began to arrive, the hammers were still going.

I held a pre-production meeting with the sheriff's department, the California Highway Patrol, and ABC, the state alcoholic beverage commission. The ABC said they'd have checkers at the event. Checkers are people who blend in with the crowd and monitor sales to ensure no liquor is sold to minors. There was something else, he advised.

"There can be no pubic hair exposed at any time."

"I'll keep my pants on at all times," I said.

That didn't end it. Despite the fact that we made our purpose clear and checked our staffing with the authorities and agreed to everything they could think of, they never did ease up. At the end of the meeting, I was notified a SWAT team would be posted in the area.

"Swell," I said.

At least God smiled down on us. The day of the concert the weather was beautiful. The sun was bright and warm, and it looked like we were going to be ready on time. The crew had camped out on the site, so I woke them early in the morning and got them going. We worked like crazy to finish up and we were ready. We just made it as the first bikes came roaring up, followed by the police. If anything happened, I would be held responsible, but as it turned out everything went smoothly.

They were the hardest people on earth to please perhaps, but even the Angels who were there had good things to say. The highest compliment of all, of course, is that it was just like the old days, and we got that. The police told me it was well organized and well done. We gave them some of our tee-shirts to take home.

When it was over, all I wanted to do was find the nearest bar, have a drink, and wind down. It had been a hectic time. As I was sitting at the bar in town, Randy Forester and Chrisco thanked me for a great time. Randy had helped a lot. So did Chrisco, a member of the Sons of Hawaii MC, an outlaw club.

Chrisco's mother owned the Silver Peso in Larkspur, California, and he became a bartender at the joint. It's near where Janis used to live, and where Vicky lives today. Randy moved to Clear Lake, which is getting pretty crowded with retirees now.

Greg Allman.

A couple of weeks later we had a great post production party at the next site for my next concert, a private airport in Petaluma. Greg Allman, of the Allman Brothers, came to the party. I wanted his band for the next concert, along with Santana, and an air show with the skydivers who had awed the crowd at the Pt Reyes show. Greg said it was one of the best parties he had been to, even if he could not remember his name. He partied so much that he almost got his ass beaten by some Hell's Angels. He went up to one of the Angel's wives and said, "Drive me home."

"Drive yourself home."

"Don't you know who I am?"

"Not a clue."

"I was married to Cher," Greg said.

"Have Cher drive you home then."

Move to Washington, D.C.

In June of 1995, Donna and I decided to leave California for Washington D.C., where I could continue my lobbying activities. I called Jerry and suggested we get together to have a picture taken of him, Cliff, and myself. In all our years, we never had a photo of the three of us. Jerry wasn't home, so I called Cliff to see if he could reach him.

"John, you'll be back," he said. I sensed I would never see Jerry again. That thought bothered me, and I shook it off as soon as I could.

And so we went to Washington.

Donna and I were barely settled into our new digs in Alexandria, when I suggested that we go for a ride on the bike. We headed for Leesburg. I'd heard there was a biker bar where we might stop before going on to Harper's Ferry. It took a while to find the bar. It was called Payne's Biker Bar. Really. There was no one inside, except a woman bartender. Donna ordered a glass of wine, and I had a beer.

"Where are you guys from?" she asked.

"Frisco."

"Live here now?"

"Just moved." The bartender excused herself to go out and put money in her meter. She came back, and we ordered another drink. A few minutes later, a guy came in and sat at the end of the bar. Over the next 10 minutes, two more guys came in and sat at the bar. When I looked at the front door, there were three angry-looking guys standing there. One stood next to Donna, and one stood right behind me. The third one, an old timer, slid up next to me at the bar.

"Are you a Hell's Angel?"

"No."

"Do you support the Hell's Angels?"

I glanced around and saw the guy behind me had his buck knife out. What the hell? My first thought was that I had to keep Donna out of harm's way, but I couldn't get a read on these guys or their problem, if there was one.

"Do you support the Hells Angels?" the old guy repeated.

"Yes, I do," I said.

"Not here you don't."

"Why's that?"

"This is Pagan territory." He flashed his tattoo.

"Where's your patch?" In most motorcycle clubs, it's mandatory to wear your patch if you're on your bike.

"We don't have to show you no patch." OK, he'd seen one too many Humphrey Bogart movies.

"Look, maybe you just better tell me what's your problem."

"I was in Frisco, the Hell's Angels drug me out of a bar and kicked the shit out of me," he explained.

"Man, that's between you and the Hell's Angels." I was getting a little nervous now, because I had heard the Pagans were bad news. There was a chance I could have a knife in my back any second, but my big concern was to get Donna out of there. She didn't seem as worried about that as I did, because she stood her ground and stared right back at the Pagan next to her.

Eventually they escorted us outside and let us go. When we got outside, I saw my "Support Your Local Hell's Angels" sticker was scratched off my fender.

The pieces fell into place then. When the bartender went out to attend to her parking meter, she saw my sticker and concluded I was a Hell's Angel and called the Pagans. The Pagans had heard some news that the Angels were moving into their territory. I'm certain if I had been an Angel, they would have killed me. I didn't realize how lucky we had been until I found out later the Pagans had nailed a woman to a tree for holding back $20 dollars from them.

CHAPTER FIFTEEN

1995 – An Unfinished Life.

Remember how I tried to get a photo of Jerry, Cliff, and myself before Donna and I left California? If I have one regret in my life, it's that I never made that happen. The three of us, who grew up and grew old together, never had our picture taken as a group. A month after Donna and I moved to Washington, D.C., I discovered that would never happen.

The news came, the way a lot of bad news comes these days, with a phone call. Oley, who worked for the Dead's sound department, phoned me early in the morning. Oley's voice was trembling.

"Jerry died," he said simply. At first it did not register.

"Jerry died," Oley repeated.

It suddenly struck me he was talking about Jerry Garcia. At the same time, it also struck me that he had to be kidding. Oley liked to play jokes, but when I listened carefully, it was obvious it was not a joke, but the end. I managed to ask Oley about the details, and he said they thought it was a heart attack, and that it occurred while he was at Forest Knolls.

Forest Knolls! Forest Knolls was about five miles from where we had just moved from, and it was very much like Lompico, where Jerry and I had spent so many good times as kids. It was where I had learned about Jerry's secret fear.

I tried to call Cliff, but got only his answering machine. I dialed Rock Sculley, who was in upstate New York, finishing his book, Living with The Dead.

"Have you heard?"

"I did. Real bummer." Even though Rock had been drummed out of the Grateful Dead organization, he always cared about Jerry. Rock is a man of many hurts, and that's what Jerry saw in him. The first time Rock saw the Dead, he told me he was going to manage that group.

"Rock, let me know if you are going to the funeral," I said.

"I will, John."

We hung up, and I tried to call Cliff again, but he wasn't in or wasn't picking up his phone. I was worried about Cliff, so I called a friend of mine and asked him to go over to Cliff's house to see if everything was all right. A short time later he called me back and said no one was home.

I was finally able to reach Cliff the next day. He had been in Santa Cruz with his family, and the news about Jerry came to him in an even more cruel way.

Cliff, his wife, and children were in a Denny's when they overheard a group at the next table talking about Jerry's death. He'd heard a lot of those rumors before, so Cliff didn't think much about it. They finished eating and returned to their car. Cliff turned on the radio and he discovered Jerry's death was not a rumor.

News reports that day were filled with grand pronouncements of his influence on popular music worldwide, of his status as an icon on the American cultural landscape, and glowing accounts of his sold-out concerts, his millions of "Dead Heads" fan base, and a lot more. The reports and sound bites were glowing, respectful, and some were even reverent in tone. The world was remembering him as all these things, an awesome, bigger-than-life man whose music went to, and remained, at the core of American young people, people who would never forget him.

It was different with me.

What I remembered was the good-natured little guy I found sitting in my secret spot at the Central Pharmacy in 1947, who lived on Harrington Street. We were combat veterans, having fought the War of the Big Kids together, me as General, him as Private. We raided back yard fruit trees together on warm summer nights, and consumed hundreds of comics in his room, as he created a world of fantasy in his sketchbooks.

Not just an icon, he was the kid who walked to school with me, dug a fort with me, rode on the back of my first bike, learned to ride horses together, and cleaned stables with side-by-side.

He was the funny little kid, who had a grandma named Tillie and a parrot in the kitchen. We went swimming in the salt-water pools at Sutro Baths, and rode the merry-go-round while Laughing Sal cackled over us.

I remembered these things in the first instant I knew he was gone, and they live with me still, indelible and as lasting as my breath.

In Washington, D.C., word spread quickly there would be a tribute to Jerry at the Lincoln memorial that night. I joined the massive crowd there. There were tearful people, television cameras and everywhere, candles flickering in the twilight, fighting the darkness that enveloped our hearts. Here were thousands of people mourning the passing of a man who had influenced and perhaps changed their lives.

And here I was, an old and lonely friend. To be sure, I cried, because among the throng, the cruel, penetrating realization that Jerry was really gone plunged into my heart. I walked around, milling with the crowd, and talked with some of the tear-stained kids, who told me they felt they had lost a family member, a leader, and a caretaker of their souls.

But there was a flicker in them, a small fire Jerry had lighted in their lives and which would keep them warm and give them illumination and strength. He gave all of that – and the enduring message of peace and love.

But, wait, there's more.

About a month after Jerry's death, Donna brought home a CD, "Blue Incantation," by Sanjay Mishra with Jerry Garcia. Our Jerry Garcia? I had never heard of it, but when we listened, it was remarkable. Inside the cover was a telephone number for Sanjay. The area code was the same as ours! I called. Sanjay lived three miles from us in Falls Church.

I invited Sanjay over to the house, and I asked him how he had connected with Jerry. He told us he met him in October 1994, at the Washington, D.C. Headquarters of Greenpeace, where he was working at the time. There's some intrigue to the story.

A woman called Greenpeace for some information and left a return number to have someone call her at the Four Seasons Hotel. Sometimes calls like this were suspicious because no one knew this woman, nor whom, if anyone, she represented.

Without being not entirely paranoid, there was good reason to be cautious about corporate spies seeking information that could be used against the organization and its aims. Sanjay drew the assignment of calling the woman back to arrange an appointment.

"When the day came to meet her, I looked out the window and saw Jerry Garcia," he explained with great animation. He recognized Jerry right away and was very excited because he was a great fan. When Jerry came inside, they talked about the environment, the condition of the planet, and other mutual concerns.

"I felt very comfortable in Jerry's presence, so much so that I gave him a copy of my latest recording, "The Crossing" released on a small-company label.

Jerry put the disc in his pocket and left. Sanjay felt he'd never see Jerry again, but when he called the next day to follow up on some information, Jerry picked up the phone and immediately began telling him how much he enjoyed his music. Then came the shocker.

"How can I play a part in your next recording?" Sanjay verified he was serious and they arranged to record something together. Sanjay offered to book any recording studio in the world, and Jerry suggested they record at the Grateful Dead Studios in San Rafael.

"This one's on me," he said. "Just bring tape."

Not realizing the tape line was a joke, Sanjay showed up at the Dead Studios, and the first thing Jerry wanted to know was what was in the boxes that he had shipped in advance.

"Why... it's tape."

Jerry laughed and explained the joke. After the recording session, Sanjay talked with Jerry many times on the phone and the result of their collaboration was "Blue Incantations." This alliance was remarkable, because Jerry seldom did side projects with other artists, and when he did, it was almost never at the Grateful Dead Studio.

Jerry and Sanjay talked about doing another recording, and Jerry expressed an interest in going to India some time. He promised him he'd find the time, and

Sanjay was thrilled. It was the last time they spoke. .

After Jerry's death, Sanjay planned a trip to India, and extended an invitation to Deborah Koons, Jerry's widow. Deborah and some of her friends accepted his offer. What followed was not a big surprise. They told Sanjay they wanted to put some of Jerry's ashes in the Ganges River.

Recovering from his surprise, Sanjay picked a spot on the Ganges that was considered most auspicious. The name of the town is Rishikesh. There, with solemnity and decorum, some of Jerry's ashes were put into the Ganges. That took place on the day following a full moon, on the day of Buddha's birth.

I told Sanjay some of Jerry's relatives were upset that a portion of his ashes was put into India's sacred river. This was upsetting to the quiet, gentle man. He sent a bottle with some water from the Ganges to Cliff.

Cliff liked that.

AFTERWORD

The summary of a man's life often may be found by tracking the paths he's walked, and the friends he makes during his days. In the peaks and valleys of our lives, Fate stands beside the path, laughing. Many people came to know Jerry Garcia as a man. My privilege was to know him throughout the entire journey of his life.

We shared a childhood together that was something quite special, not because Jerry went on to become famous or rich or a cultural icon, or the spiritual leader of a generation. It was special because we were two kids living on the same block, who grew up building forts, reading each other's comic books, and shoveling horse stables side-by-side. We peered at life from inside the safety of our imaginary world and then ran outdoors, and in a series of glorious, golden days, explored much of it together.

Every man's boyhood is shared more intensely with a friend than with parents, relatives, teachers, or anyone else. Perhaps the story of the 60-foot cross on Mt. Davidson in San Francisco, the one that seemed to watch over us as we adventured on Harrington Street, sums up the lives of Jerry Garcia and John Clark as much as anything. In the mid-90s atheists went to court to have the cross-torn down, basing their demand on the argument that the city-maintained structure violated the separation of church and state.

Arguments and counter-suits resulted. Finally, the City and County of San Francisco held an auction and sold the cross and the one-third acre of land on which it stands to a private organization. They promptly posted signs around the area that the cross and land are "not owned or maintained by the City and County of San Francisco." That wasn't enough; lawsuits are still being filed to remove that rugged old cross.

In 60 years it went from being a friendly guardian of two small boys in a neighborhood, to a controversial icon of its own. Jerry would not have been pleased. He believed in friendship, not conflict, joy, not despair, music not politics. In the end, it is conceivable Jerry's music will outlive the stone cross. in which case, how grateful will be the dead?

Jerry's at peace. It's the world that is still filled with tumult and shouting, and music that is of the streets and not of the heart. The streets that Jerry helped fill with with music and meaning, await someone like him whose talent and commitment can ignite us, not in flames, but in a gentle warmth that illuminates the spirit without the penalty of pain.

Life itself is a terminal disease. The others in this story, who may have touched your heart, should be accounted for. I do that now as well as I am able.

Cliff Garcia still works for Dead enterprises. He lives in Marin County with his wife, Gayle, and three children. Thanks, Cliff, for being my friend, for the guitar lessons I never mastered, and for our years together.

After spending some time in a rest home, Jerry and Cliff's grandmother and guardian, Tillie, died in 1974. She understood kids, and believed they should have a nap after lunch. She was a great lady.

Papa Ralph is married, lives in Stockton, and still rides like in the old days. We used to spend quite a bit of time together before I moved to back east. I miss you both, Ralph and Lou. Ralph, you've been my friend for all these years, and, no, I don't have a window for you.

Ray Hahn ("Howdy Doody") was killed in Fresno, California while riding a bicycle. A bicycle. I miss you like the world, Howdy.

Bob Kauffman still rides. He lives on a ranch in the Sierras. I can imagine Bob on his bike, tooling twisty mountain roads on quiet days, remembering. We also spent a lot of time together before I moved. Maybe we'll take one of those rides together sometime.

Filthy Phil doesn't ride too much anymore, but he's still as strong as ever and still friends with that Tennessee gentleman, Jack Daniels. Phil used to drop by my house all the time before I moved. Thanks, Phil, for the artichokes and the memories. Especially the latter.

Pete Page still rides, but is retired from the club. He attends functions at various MC clubhouses and is well respected. Pete, old pal, thanks for being there for me.

Bob Roberts rides as strong today as he ever did. He isn't in the club anymore, but he's highly respected and well remembered. Unforgettable? Damn straight. And again, Bob, thanks.

Colorful Mofo Chuck was riding his bike when he ran into the back of a truck. He remained in a coma for many years before he died. Chuck, I hope you weren't trying to light a cigarette when you hit the truck. We all remember and respect you.

My brother works for a San Francisco newspaper and is married to a wonderful woman. They have two kids.

My stepfather died in 1998.

My mother is in a rest home.

THE END

John Clarks Patch

John Clark and Greatful Dead Manager Rock Scully.

Made in the USA
Lexington, KY
14 March 2019